Landscape Basics

discover the basics of landscape design

Shirley Lise

Published by LISE Publishing

Box 2198 St. Marys, ON,

N4x 1A1

Landscape Basics

Copyright© 2010 by Shirley Lise

All rights reserved. No part of this book may be reproduced without permission.

All text, drawings, and photograph illustrations by Shirley Lise

Interior and Cover design by Shirley Lise

ISBN: 978-1492818113

Printed in the United States of America

Introduction

There are different reasons for putting effort into landscaping your property. Because you picked up this book, likely you have already been impressed with its value. As a home owner, you probably know that a landscaped lot is appealing to the senses if done properly, that curb appeal is enhanced, and that the monetary value of such an investment will pay off in the long run. Whether you just want to enjoy your property more fully, or plan to market it, improving your property with the addition of hardscaping as well as plantings will reap satisfying benefits.

But landscaping serves yet another purpose. It facilitates outdoor living. A well-designed driveway not only improves the curb appeal of your home, but also provides a durable surface on which to park your vehicles. The sidewalk, whether stoic or meandering in design, provides a safe pathway to the front door. Of course the journey to the front entrance is exceedingly enhanced and enjoyed when surrounded by buds and sweet smelling colorful blooms of shrubs and perennials. Even so, a beautifully designed front yard is only part of the outdoor experience. The more private areas of your property are of equal importance and, depending on your lifestyle, facilitate comfortable extended outdoor living with food preparation and dining areas at the least, and recreational spaces to include a pool, sauna, hot tub, children's play area and other features depending on the lifestyle, size of the property, and budget.. Hardscaped areas laid-out to best meet your needs, while enhanced with well-designed gardens, will give you results worth the time, effort, and investment put into it.

Landscape Basics is written as a handy reference tool to help you, as a homeowner, determine your outdoor needs and to design and implement a landscape plan that will serve your lifestyle while at the same time, contribute to the beauty, enjoyment, and value of your property.

Contents

6	The Site
8	Hardscaping
28	Water Features
31	Fences, Walls, & Gates
36	Trellises, Arbors, & Gazebos
40	Lighting
44	Style by Design
50	Flow
56	Balance
60	Good Proportion
62	Focal Point
64	Size & Shape
74	Beds & Borders
80	Adding Ground Cover
82	Designing A Walkway
92	Landscaping On A Slope
100	Selecting Trees
108	Selecting Shrubs
113	Designing With Perennials
129	Designing With Annuals
139	Garden Accents
143	The Winter Garden
148	Developing A Landscape Plan

The Site

Before a landscape plan can begin, the use of the outdoor space must be considered. Areas that will be open to the public, such as a front yard of a home or business need to be considered independently of the family living areas. The front yard directs people to the front entrance, while more private areas would include areas to cook and dine out, children's play areas, a swimming pool, outdoor fireplace or fire pit, or other entertainment areas. Similarly, areas used to service the property, such as those including a clothes line, garbage storage, dog houses, compost bins, and other storage, need to be considered apart from public and family living areas.

When landscaping around a home, the front yard, which is seen by everyone, will facilitate entry to the home via a driveway and a pathway to the front door while more private uses will be facilitated in the side or back yard of the home with layouts of hardscaping to include decks, patios, walkways, and fencing to define each space and provide necessary safety and privacy. For a hardscape plan to be successful, designated outdoor areas must coincide with indoor use. For instance, the outdoor kitchen and dining area are best situated directly adjacent to the indoor kitchen with doors opening between them for ease of flow from indoor to outdoor. Likewise, access to the pool area might be directly linked to a master bedroom for convenience.

Once the uses of the site have been determined, the site must be analysed. Its size and surroundings need to be considered and natural characteristics of land slopes, existing plantings, wooded areas, natural water features, as well as placement of existing buildings noted as well as existing hardscaping including patios, decks, pools, ponds, fences and other features you plan to work with and around. If the project is extensive, and the terrain is not suitable for its designated uses, the site may have to be altered.

Steep slopes interfering with activities and uses planned, or excessively flat areas causing drainage problems, can be re-graded and leveled suitably. Areas designated for parking, swimming pools, and sitting requiring fairly level surfaces can be altered to accommodate these uses while other areas such as those designated to flower and rock gardens may be enhanced by an existing sloping grade.

Hardscaping

Front Yard Hardscaping

To hardscape a front yard, a driveway for vehicles and a sidewalk from the driveway to the front door is essential. Materials used for these areas include brick, stone, block, concrete, asphalt, crushed stone, flagstone, gravel and wood chips. When deciding on a material for your surfaces, consider cost, durability, maintenance, and appearance.

A driveway that is used intensively is best surfaced with a hard surface material such as concrete, stone, or brick. One that is not used so intensively can be surfaced efficiently with softer materials. These include asphalt or loose aggregates such as crushed stone or wood chips which are less durable and less maintenance free, but of lower cost.

Walkway and steps to a home's entrance can be most effectively surfaced with hard materials for durability and aesthetics.

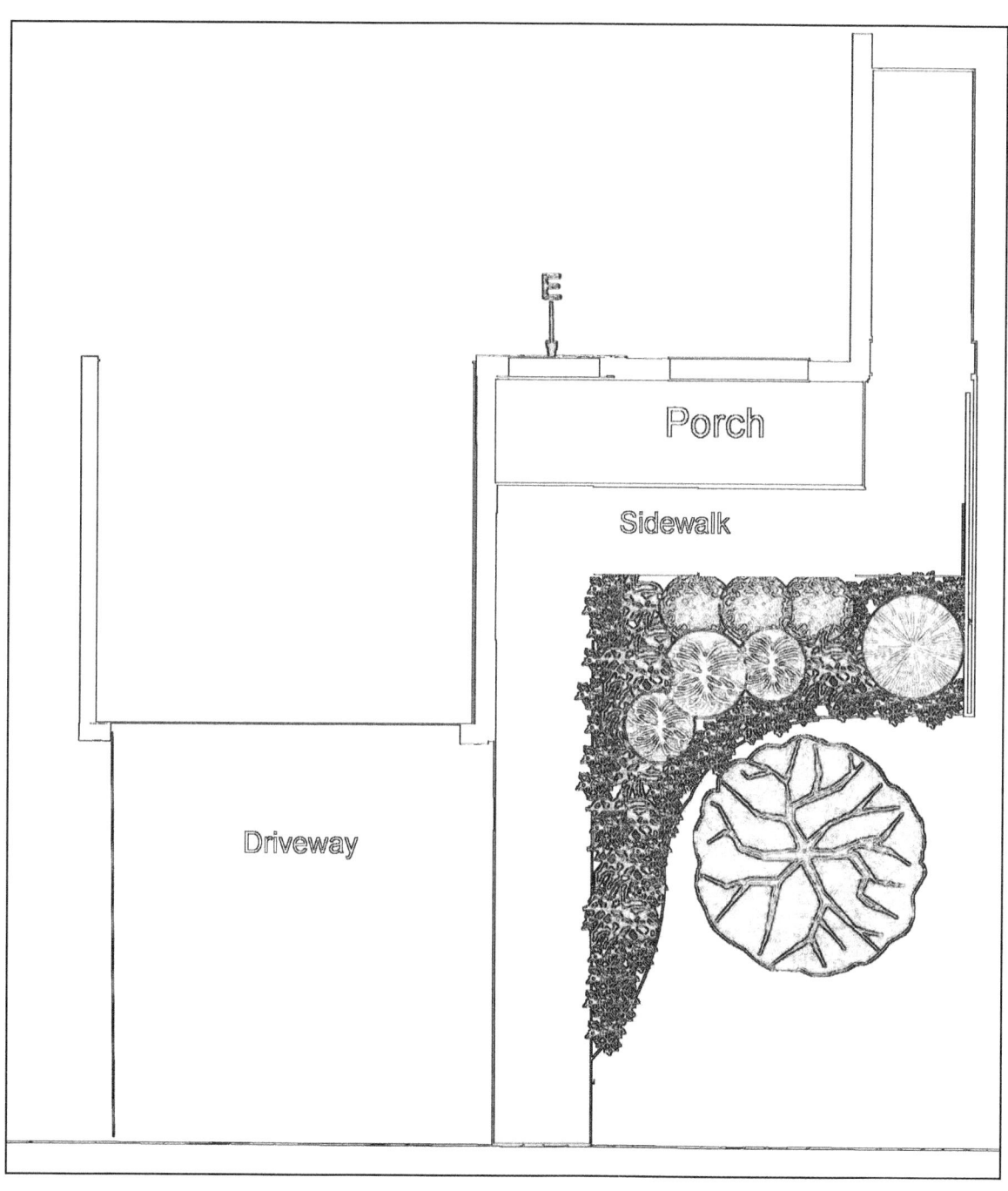

Family Area Hardscaping

The family area will include a comfortable level seating area with outdoor cooking facility. It is best located directly adjacent to the indoor cooking area for easy access to food and utensils unless an separately fully-equipped outdoor kitchen which houses outdoor cookware, cold storage, and a source of drinking water, is to be part of the plan. Best surface materials for this area are those that are durable and slip resistant.

If the entrance out from the main structure is several feet off the ground, a deck would work well. If at ground level, a patio is a better choice to avoid unnecessary steps. A combination of stepped decking along with patio adds interest as does planters and seating built in to the a multi-level deck.

Decking materials vary. Pressure treated lumber is maintenance free and cost effective, but other options are available from a local building center including wood/resin products which are longer lasting and maintenance free. Other choices in deck materials include natural woods such as cedar and cypress, which although are neither maintenance free nor cost effective, add beauty and character to the project.

A patio is best surfaced with durable hard surface materials.

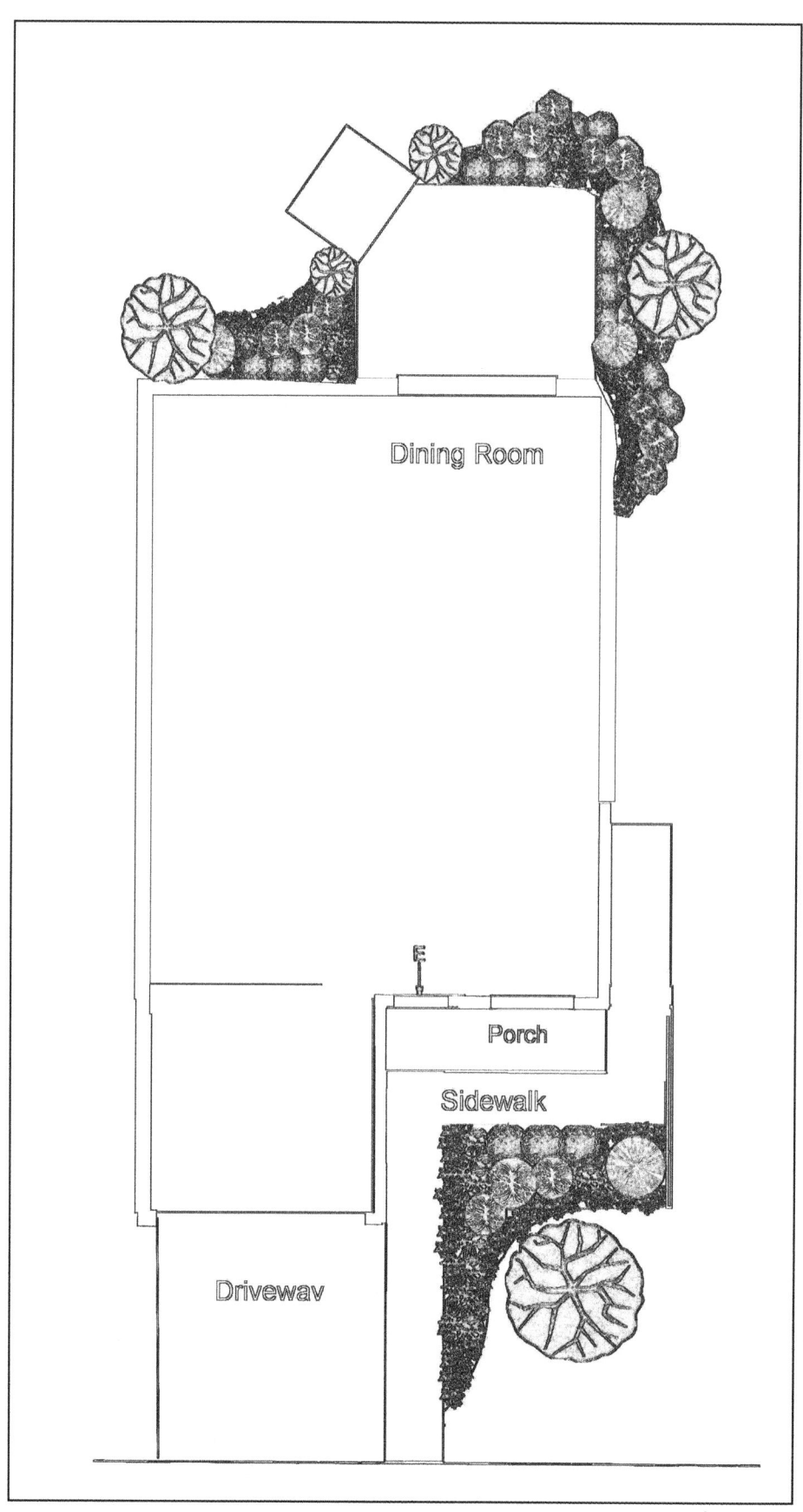

Service Area Hardscaping

Service areas can include a small patio or deck surrounded with fencing or screening to keep hidden from view garbage cans, garden potting items, and pool supplies. These areas may also incorporate a clothes line. Service areas are best located away from the public and family areas, and if possible adjacent to a back entrance for ease of use. Clothes lines should be placed where they will not interfere with walkways and gardens designed for aesthetics.

Once hardscaping of public, family, and service areas are in place, a plant design plan can begin.

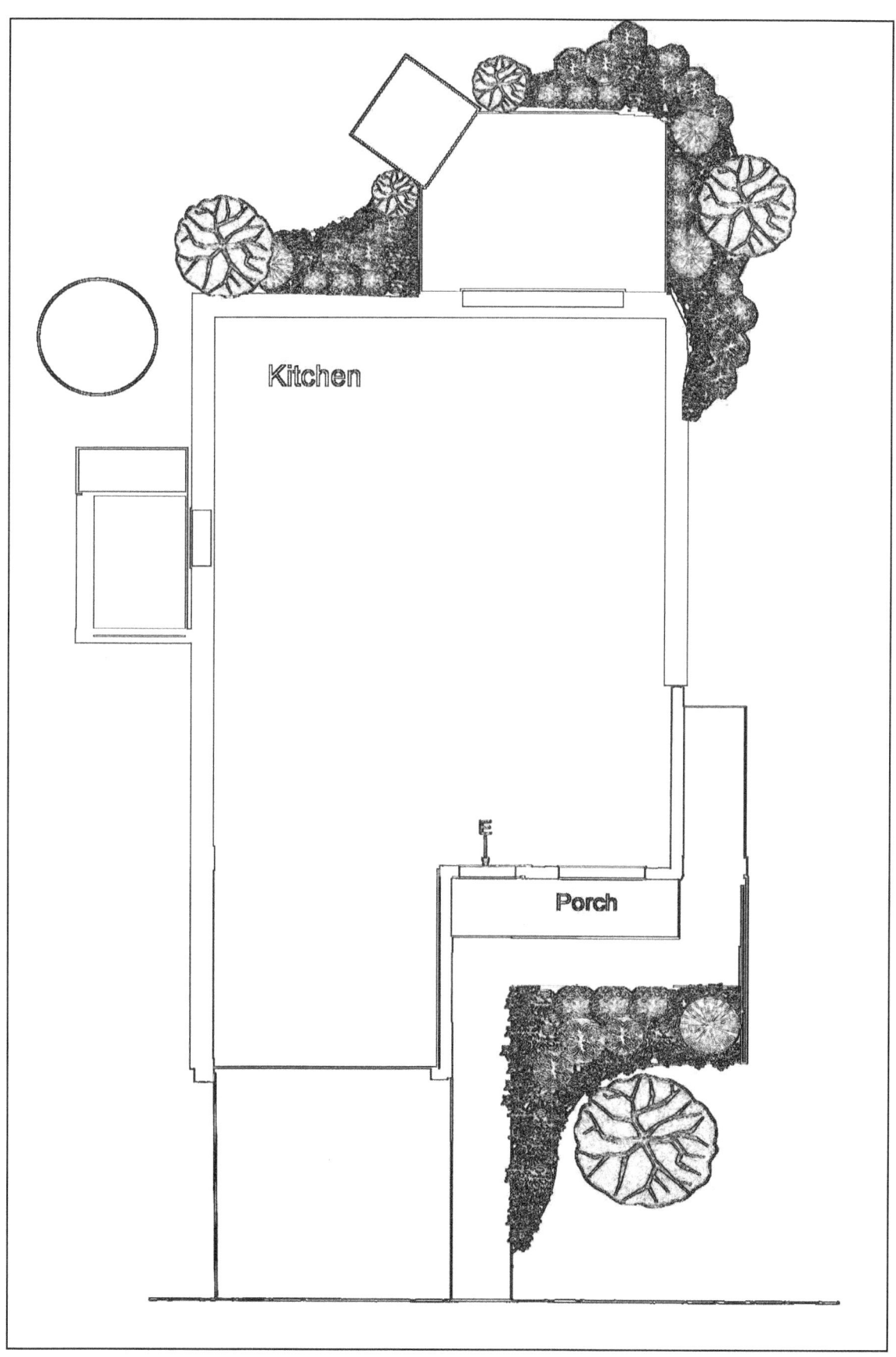

Amenities

Prior to planting, it is important to prepare for and implement the installation of amenities into your landscape plan. These will include areas designated to a hot tub, swimming pool and pool house, and patio and decking around it. If a swimming pool and hot tub is be planned for, they are most effective if worked in to the same area, and if the properly is large, away from the house. If, however, no pool is to be installed, the hot tub is better located near the house with access to a back door.

Ponds and fountains are another feature that can be added to the landscape to add the refreshing sight and sound of running water. Plantings of ornamental grasses and ferns planted around a pond naturalizes it as well as lilies growing in it. A fountain spraying out from within the pond adds another dimension of sight and sound of trickling pond water. Used as an accent feature on a patio or integrated into the garden plan, a freestanding fountain of substantial size creates an attractive focal point to the landscape.

Fences Walls & Gates

Fences and walls are effective in providing privacy. They block the wind and unpleasant sounds such as traffic driving by. They provide security. From a decorative stand point, fences and walls aesthetically add to the landscape and provide definition of a space. Enclosing a back yard with wooden fencing adds to the charm and provides a backdrop for plantings. When adding these elements to the landscape, color and style should integrate with those of the exterior of the home. Stone walls contribute a natural element, however, brick color and stained fencing should blend with a homes exterior colors.

Although gates are useful to coming in and going out of a fenced in area, they also add a decorative touch. The more detailed and the larger the gate, the more opportunity to use a gate as a focal point.

Add extra interest to your gardens and landscape with decorative trellises, an arbor or a cozy gazebo. These structures all support climbing plants and display flowering climbers to best advantage. They are helpful to provide shade and screening against wind. The gazebo, if large enough, may accommodate dining, or if scaled smaller in keeping with the dimensions of a smaller property, provides cover and may become a comfy retreat tucked into a remote corner of the yard. With all of these structures, care needs to be taken to blend their color and texture in with that of other yard structures as well as with the home itself.

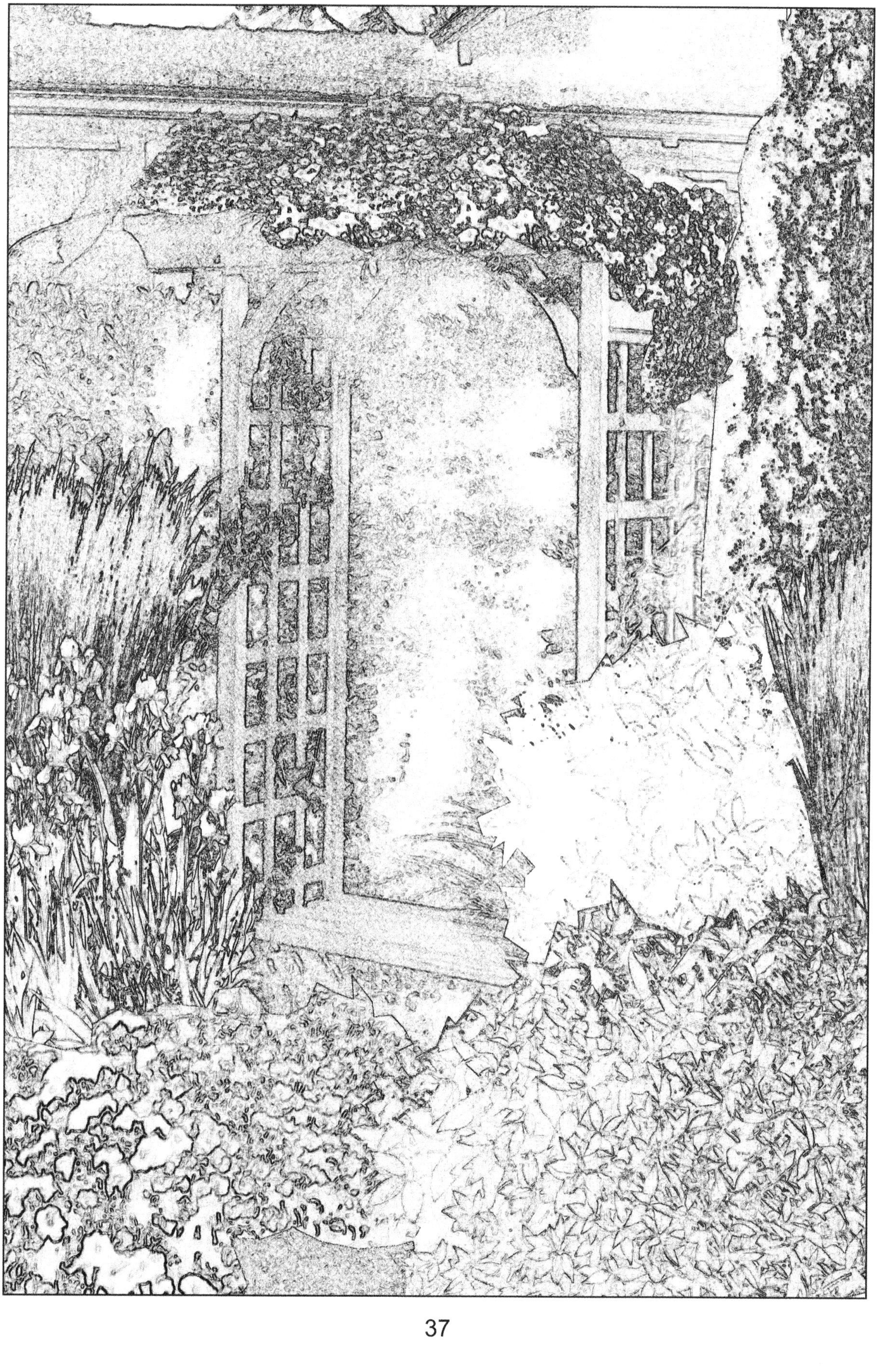

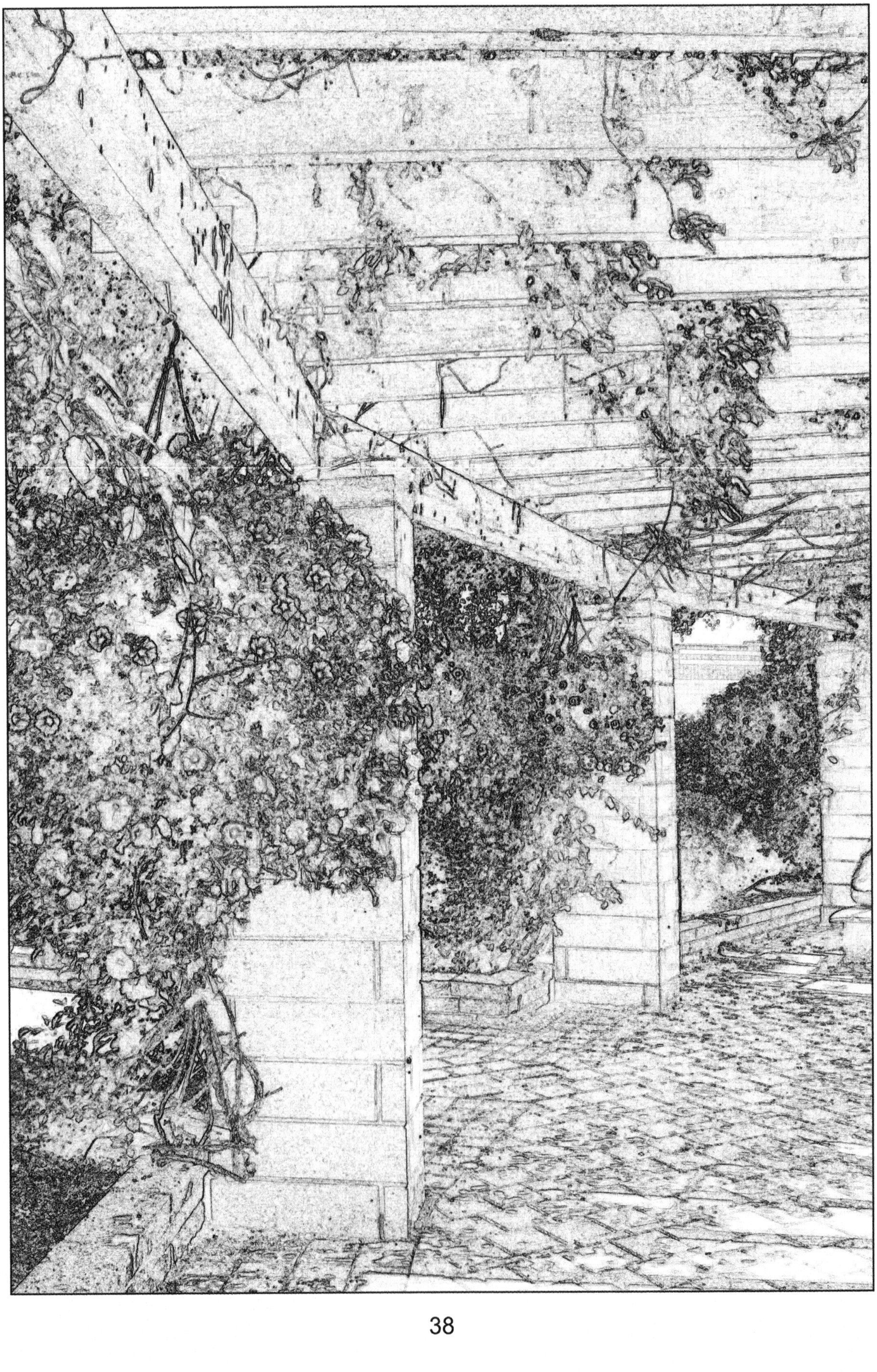

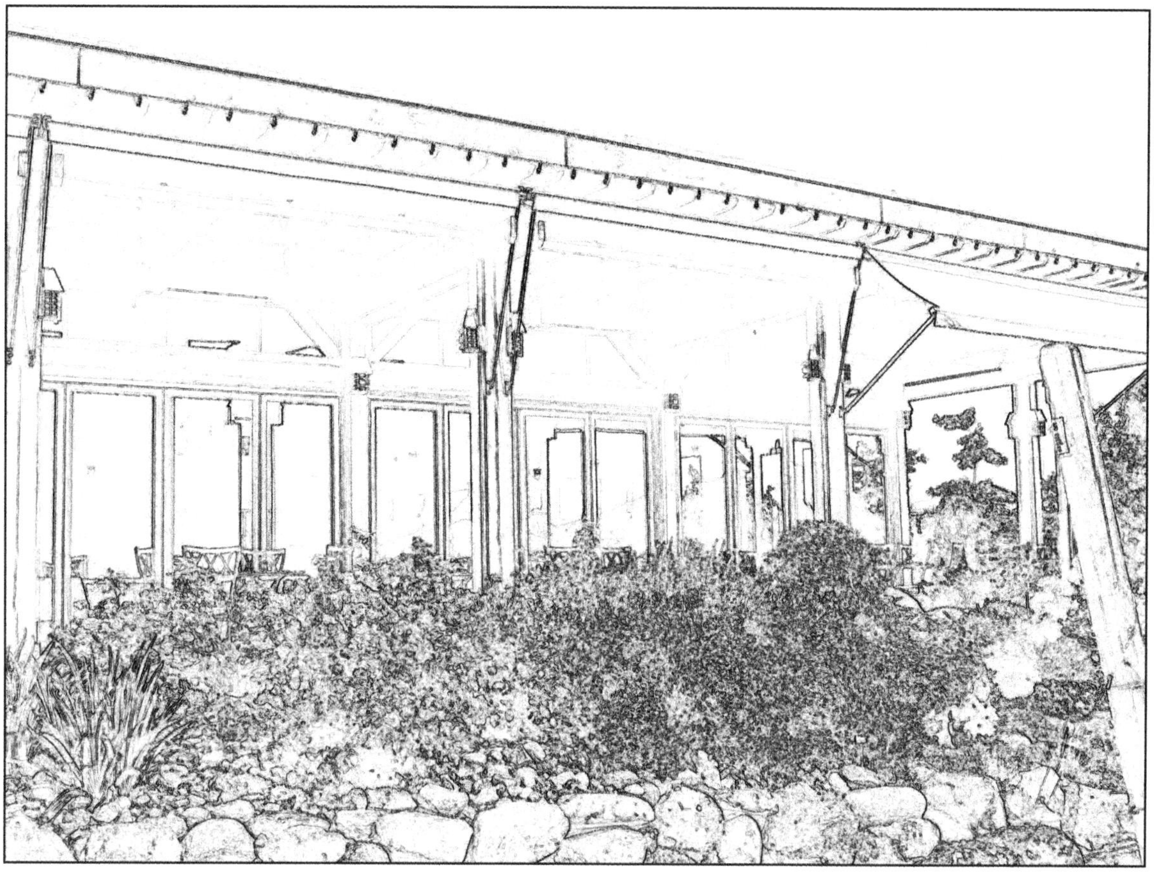

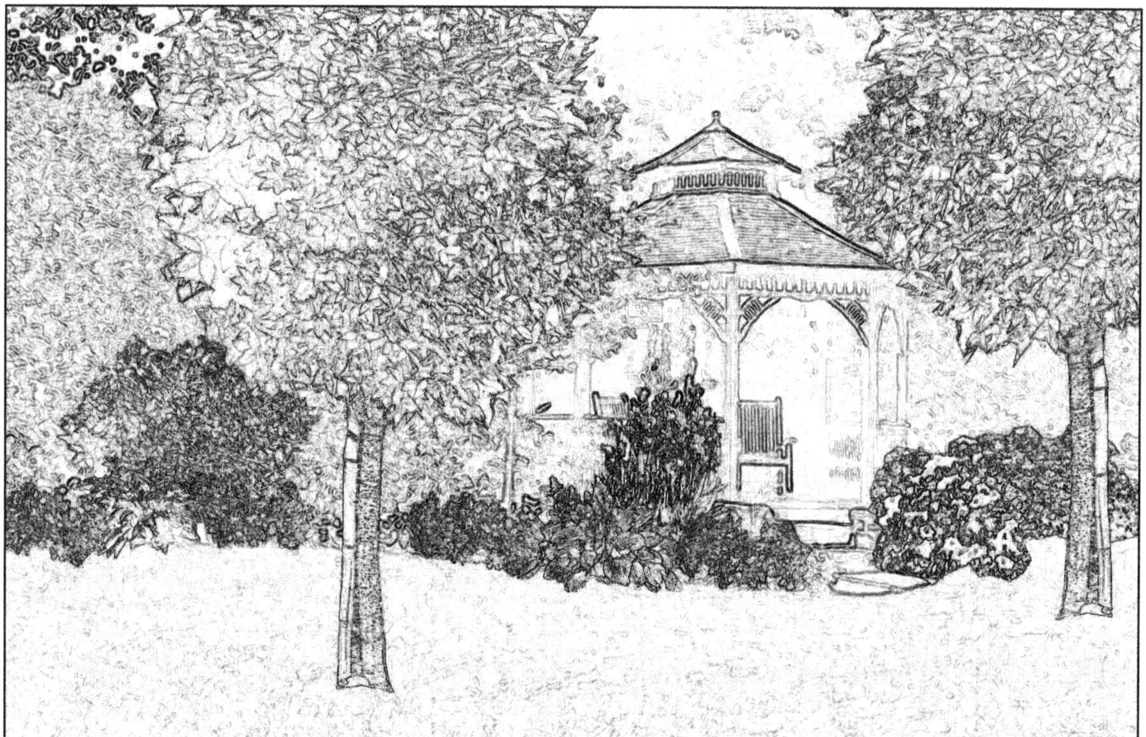

Lighting

Not only to light up stairs, walkways, and entrances for safety reasons, lighting can be used to add charm and character to an otherwise dark and dismal landscape after the sun goes down. Strategically place lamps in corners of the yard mounted on a section of fence or placed in behind a tree or shrub to back light it and wash the fence with light. To increase drama, highlight an attractive feature such as a fountain or a statue or spotlight a tree and its lower branches to form a silhouette against a wall. Plan for lighting prior to digging and have wiring installed underground and out of sight. If hard-wiring is not an option, add solar powered lighting along walkways, up deck steps, and amongst the garden for special emphasis.

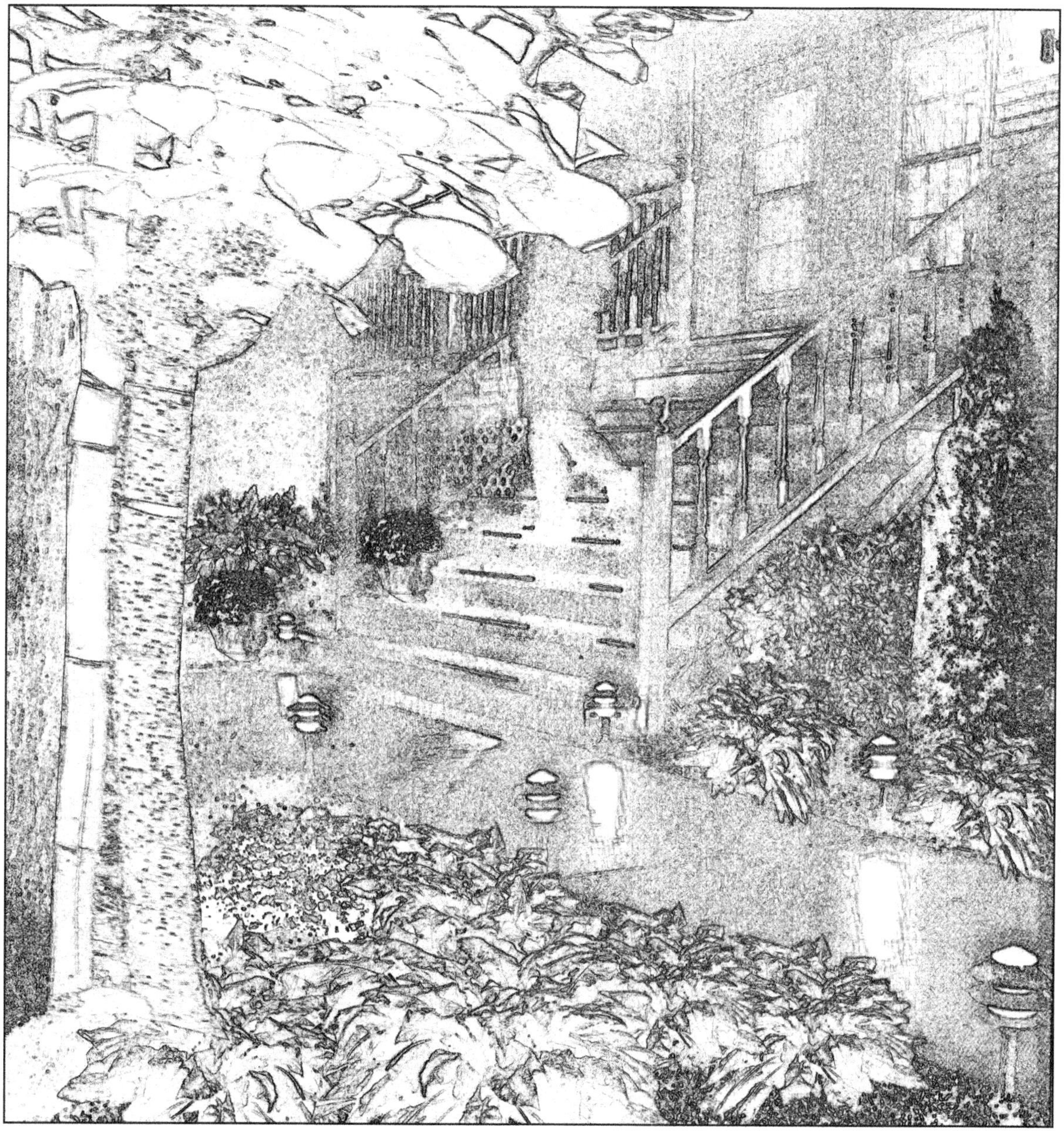

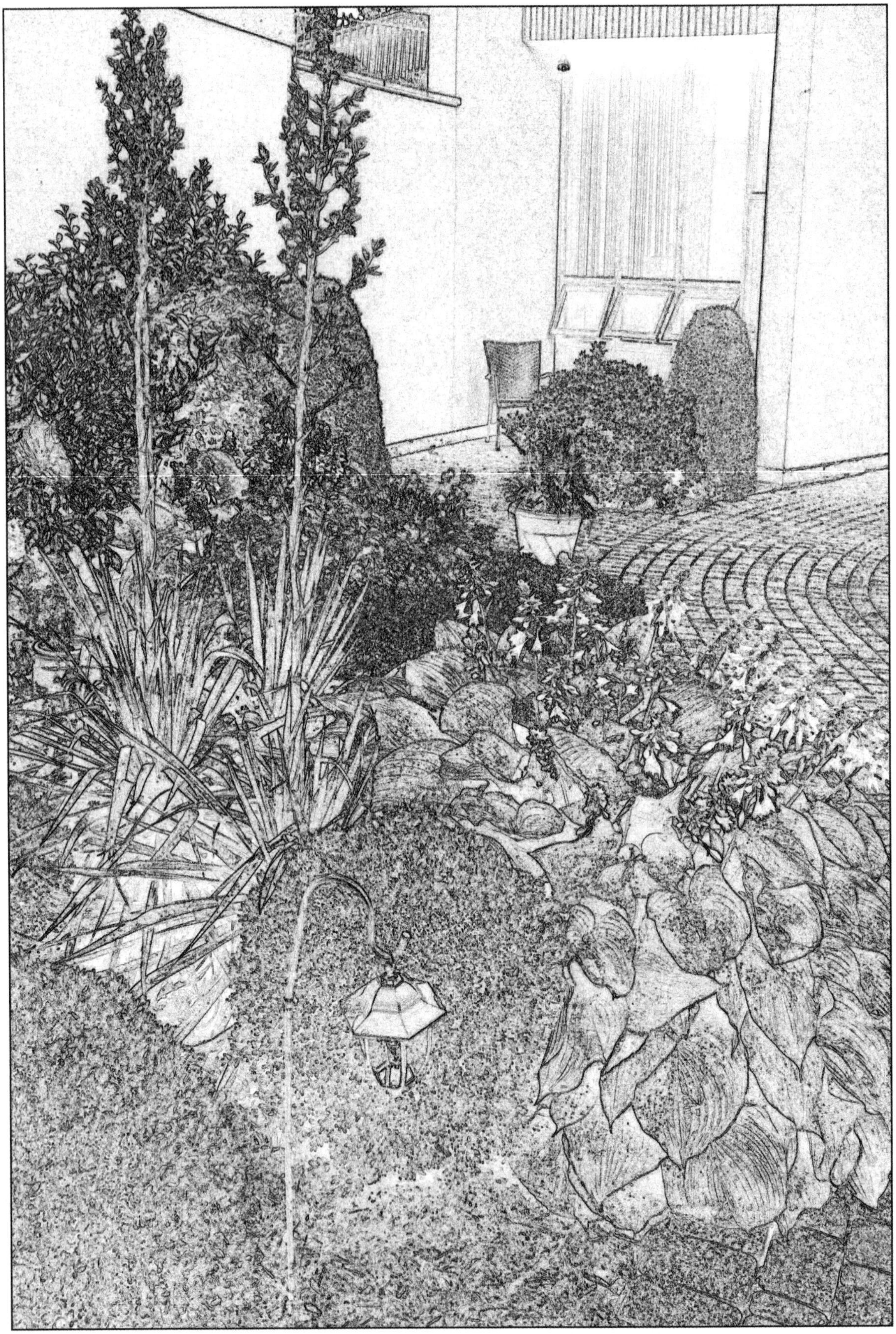

43

Style by Design

Landscaping, as decorating, gives opportunity to achieve style. All elements of the design work together in a unified way to produce a certain feeling. Color, texture, shape, and form all come into play when implementing style.

Creative flow is not limited to the design of gardens incorporated into the landscape, but is implemented with the design of the layout of the total scape, thus includes the design and strategic positioning of hardscaping as well. Patios and decks not only prove functional, but their color, shape, form and texture of materials used contribute to the style of the scheme. Rough textured materials such as stone used in a patio, retaining wall, or steps, for instance, enhance a rustic, comfortable feel, while smooth concrete used instead, contribute to a more modern design.

Creative flare can be further introduced to hardscaping by the use of rounded edges, added features, and multi-layer design. Instead of a squared-off deck, incorporate a curve for a more fluid visual look and divide deck areas into upper and lower portions by stepping it from section to section designating separate uses for each section. Build in planters and seating to more fully define each space and add even more interest to the design.

When adding plantings to the landscape, another style choice comes into play and should be equally considered. Garden styles range from formal to informal, from a "cottage garden" feel, to a more structured and manicured look. Although both can be used together, displays of tall-growing perennial grasses that sway in a breeze create a different experience than do excessive plantings of clipped yews, for example. When seeking to impart a particularly more stoic feel to the garden, consider more manicured species such as the clipped yews with a tighter, more compact shape. To achieve a less-formal look, add grasses and species of plants that are more free-flowing in nature. The garden style chosen should be coherent with the style created by hardscaping.

. Because color, texture, and shape also play an important role when working with style, decide if your garden is to be bold and colorful with splashes of bright reds, yellows, and orange blooms, or more subdued with a palette of cooler more-muted colors.

To gain unity in the landscape design as a whole, limit choices of plants to a few varieties. Group together plantings of the same variety in masses as well as repeat them throughout the landscape from one area to the next for a most harmonious display.

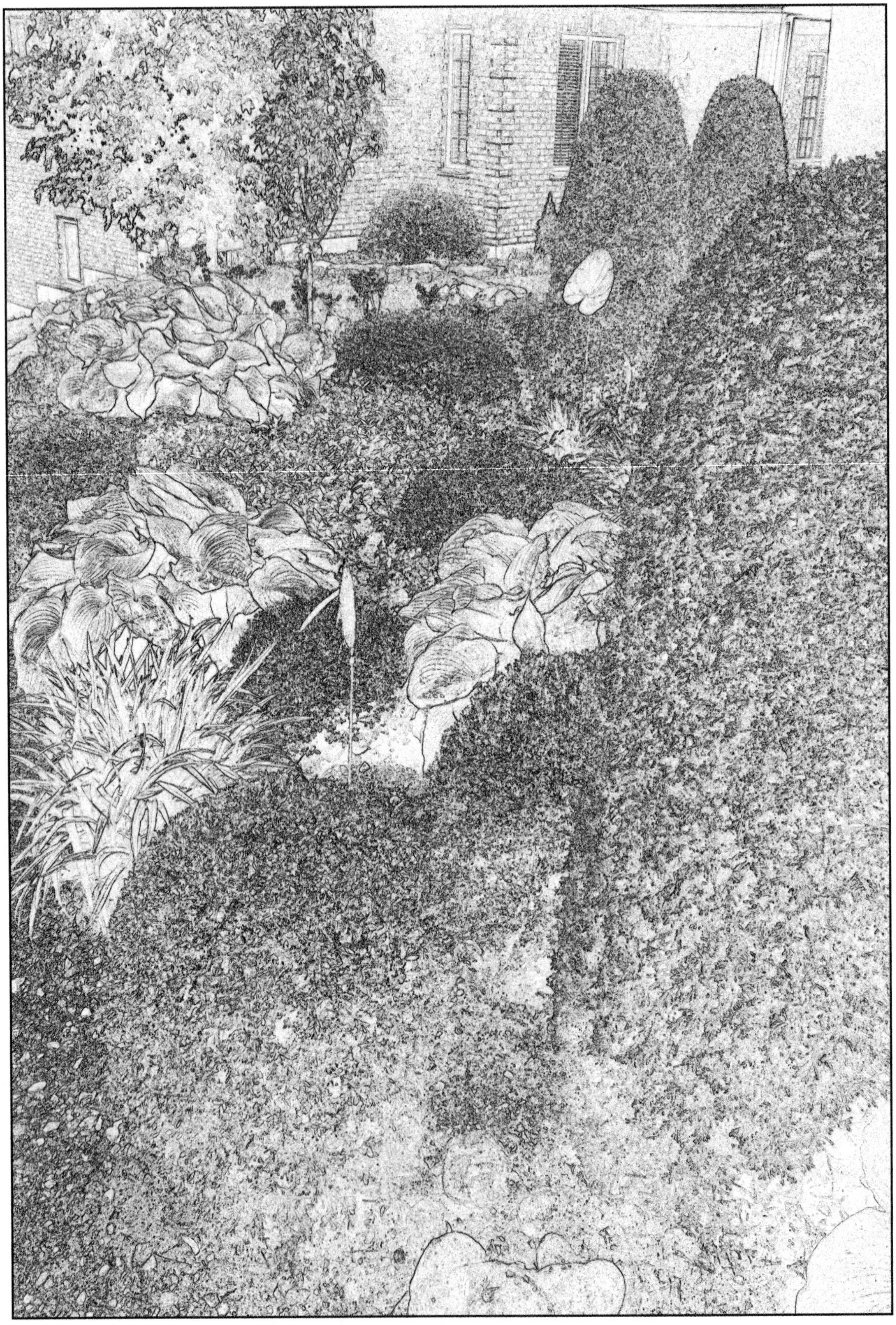

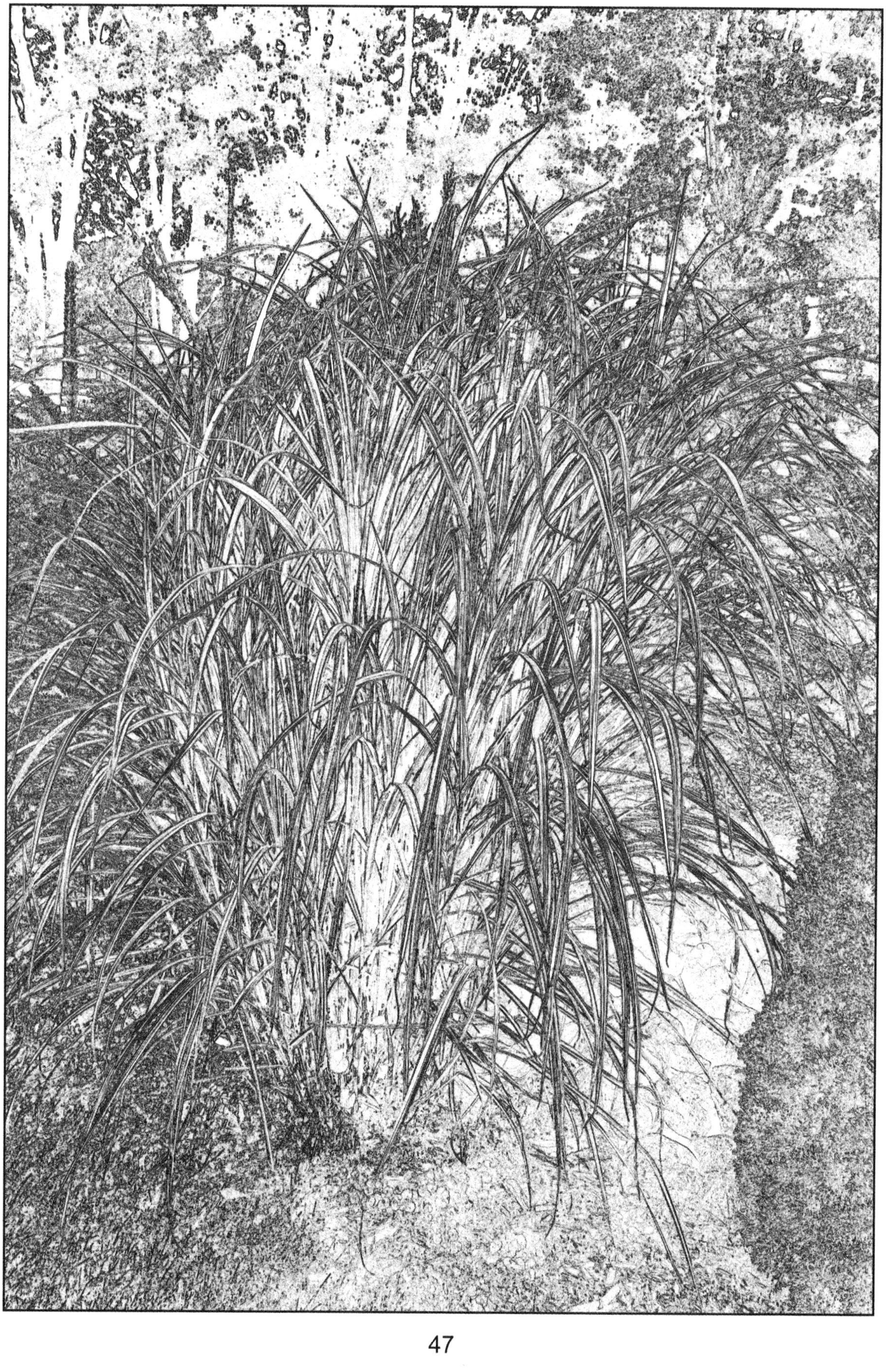

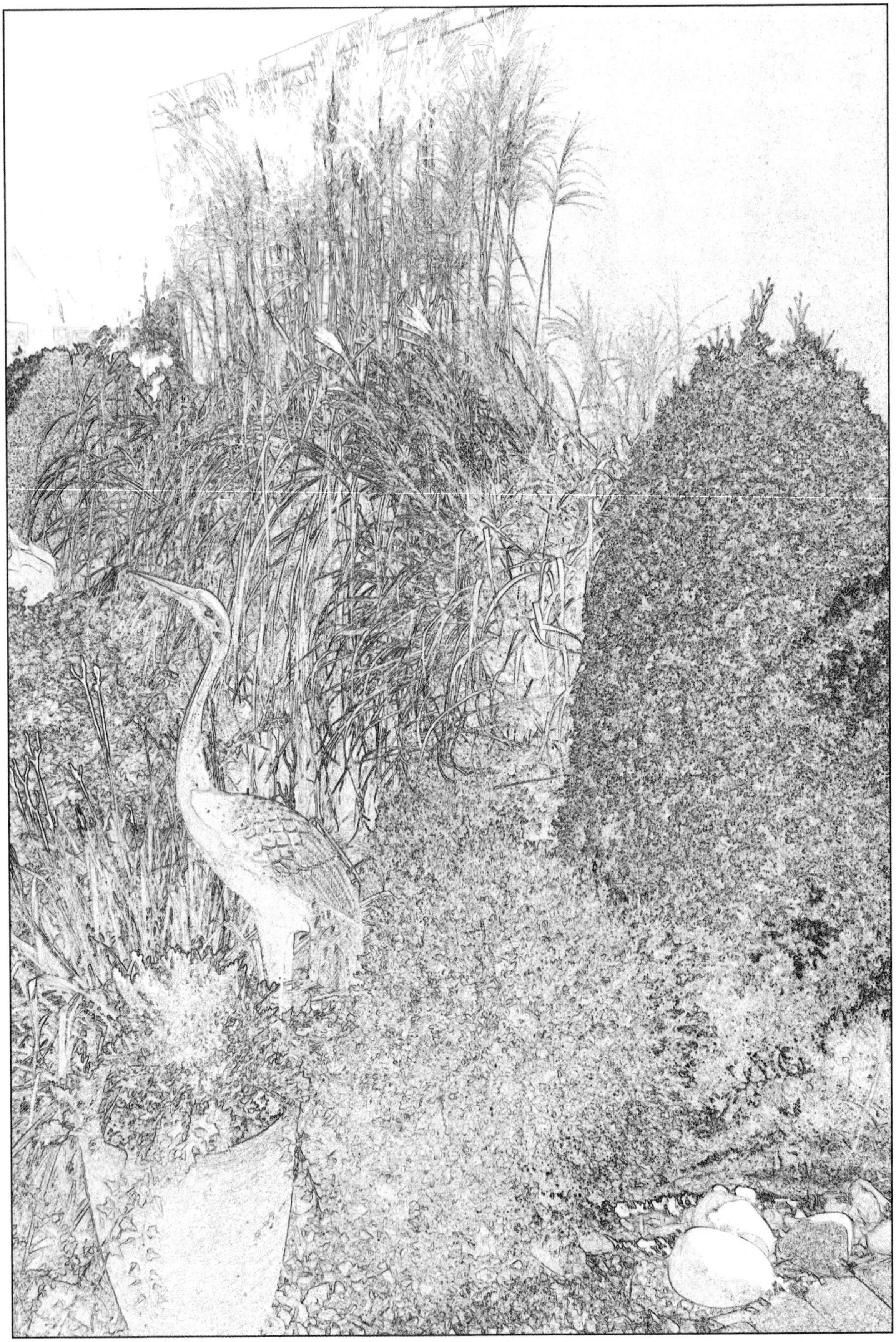

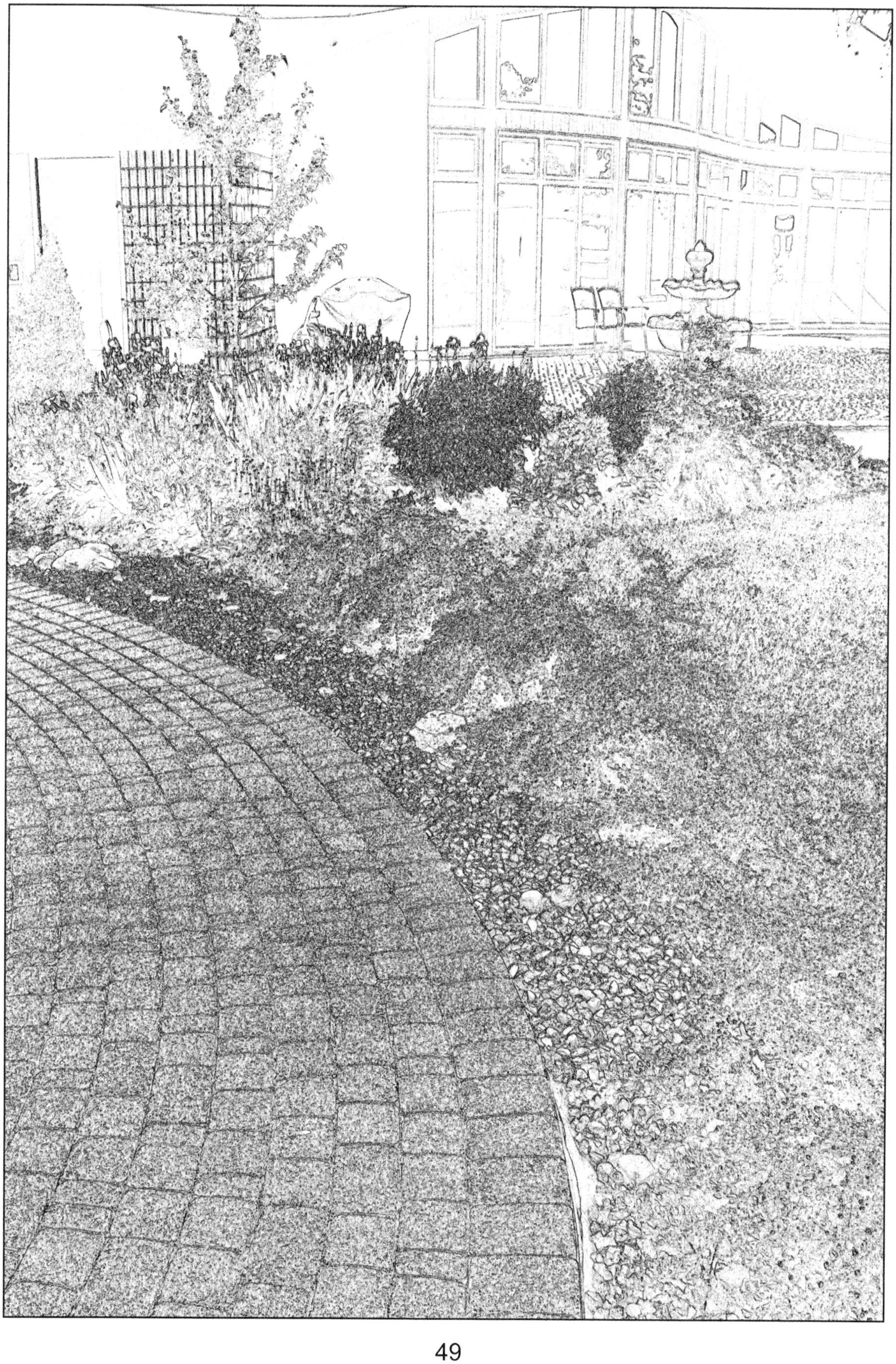

Flow

Along with style, comes flow and consistency in the design scheme. A good landscape design will create uninterrupted flow from one planting area to the next, causing the eye to follow a gently rolling landscape with gradual changes in heights and dimensions. This arrangement gives the impression of a coherent display with no abrupt changes to interrupt.

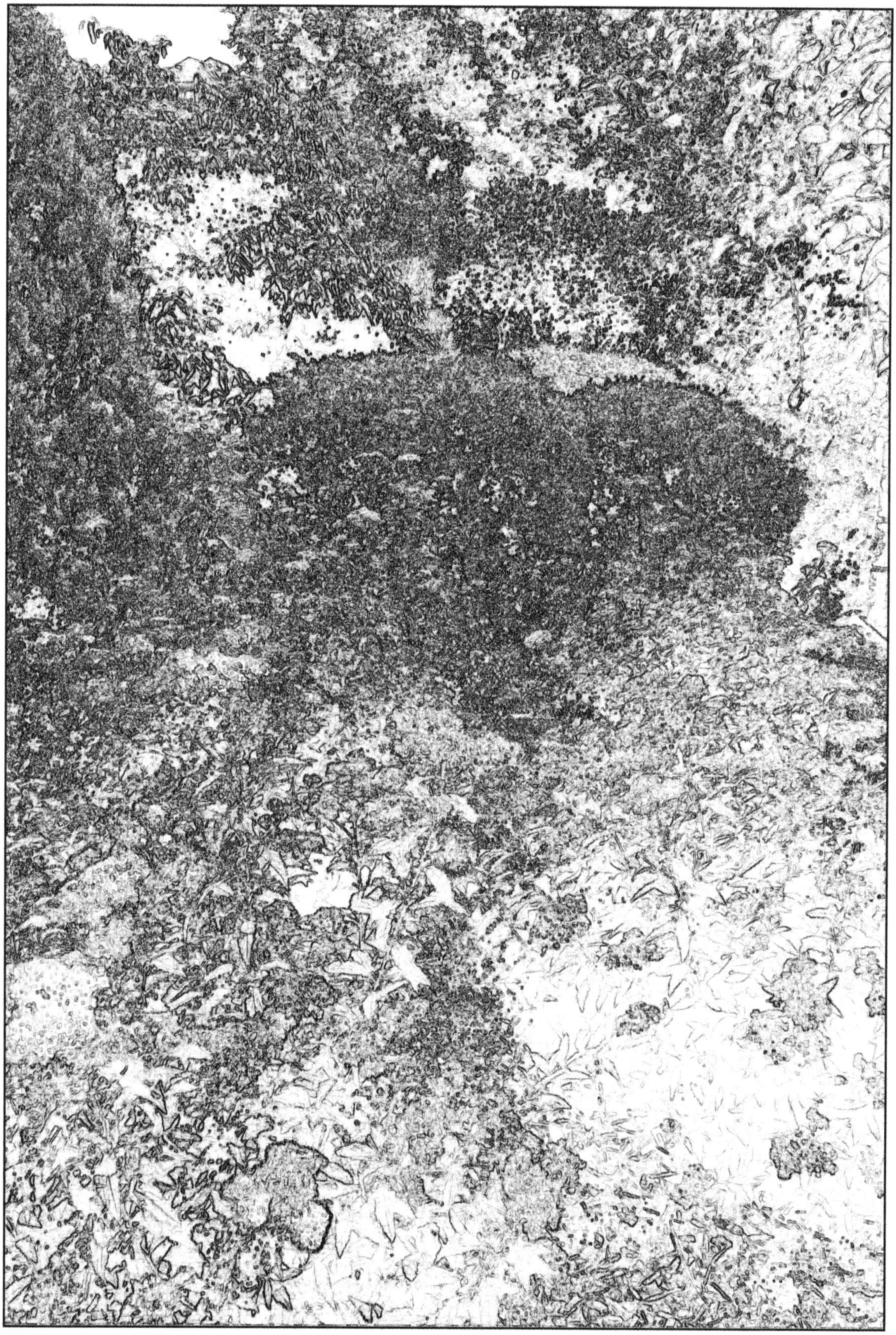

Repetition of Plantings

Repeating plant species within a garden creates unity and gives the garden a sense of uninterrupted flow. A rule of thumb is to limit the number of different species used and repeat them. This rule applies to use of color and texture as well. If you have several gardens, link them together harmoniously by repeating these elements throughout all gardens.

Massing of Plantings

Although massing plantings is a form of repetition, it further compliments a garden by grouping similar plantings together providing a less-cluttered design. By grouping similar plantings, the garden appears more restful.

Repeating plant specimens along a walkway as a form of massing, guides the eye along the path in an uninterrupted fashion. Study the following illustrations, noting repetition of plant species. Observe the massing of plant species along a walkway and how this positioning of similar plantings carries the eye along the path.

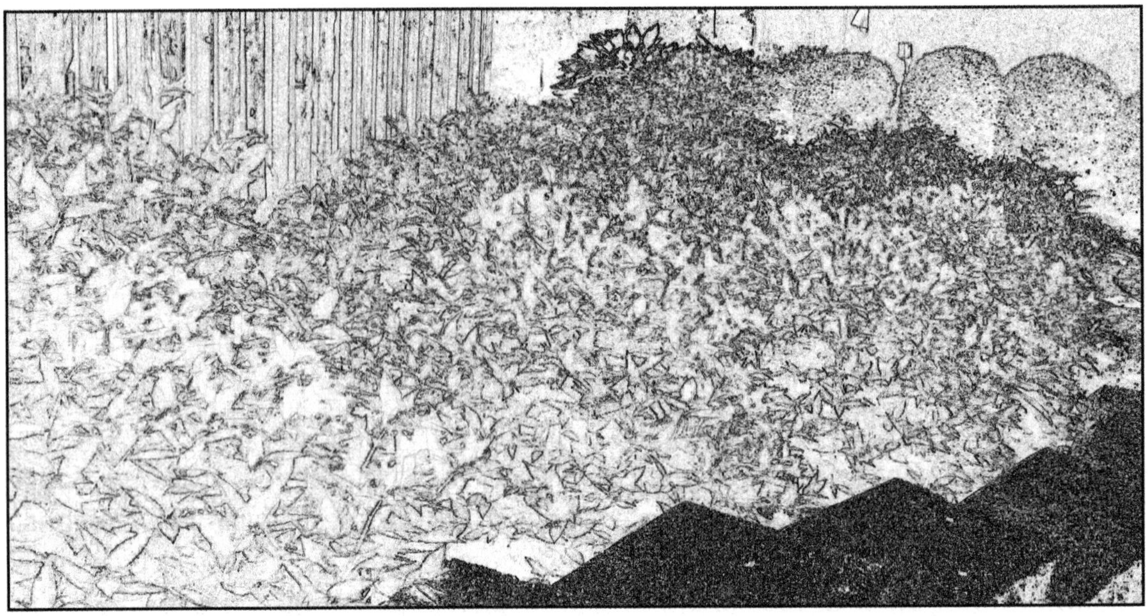

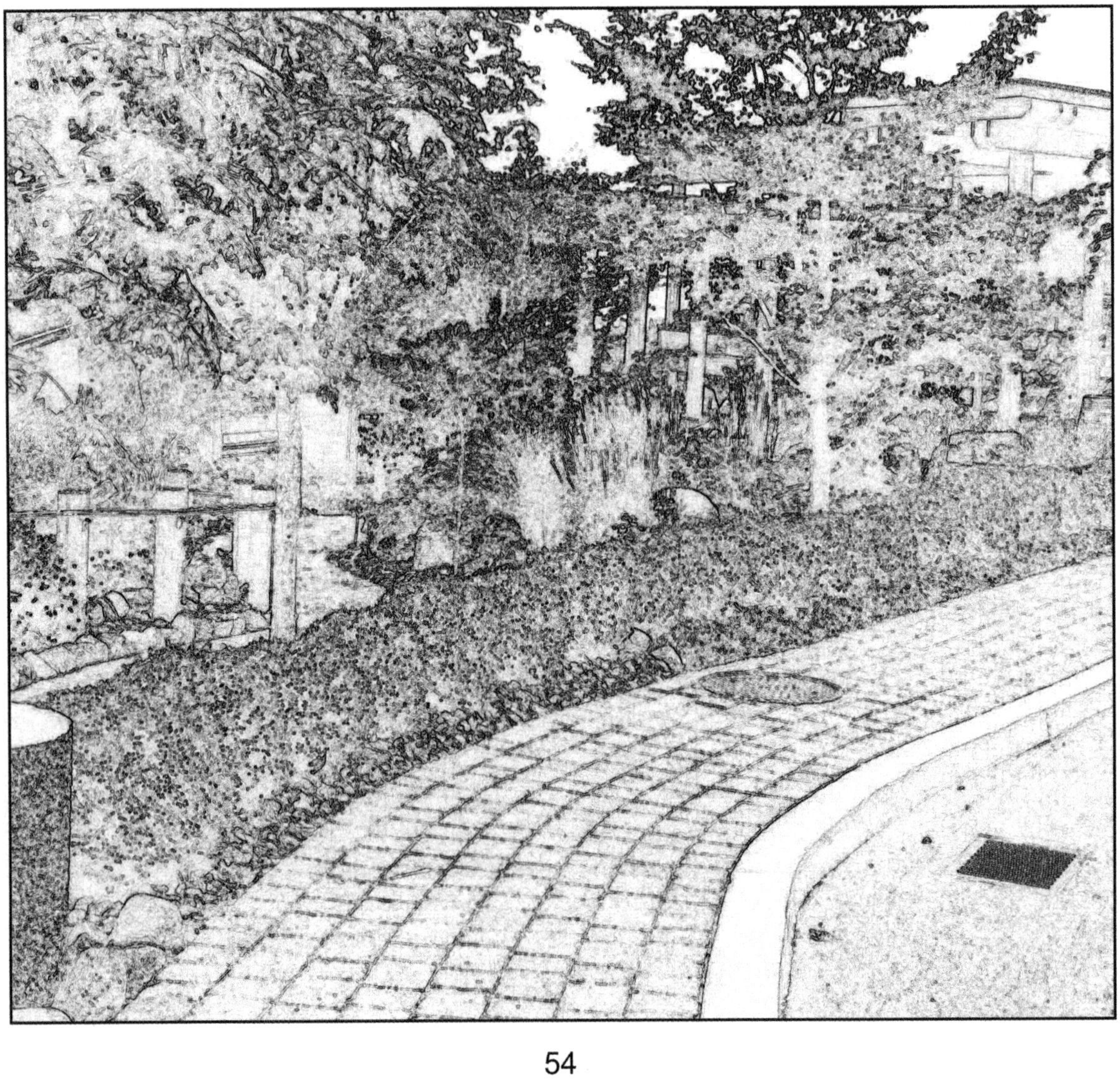

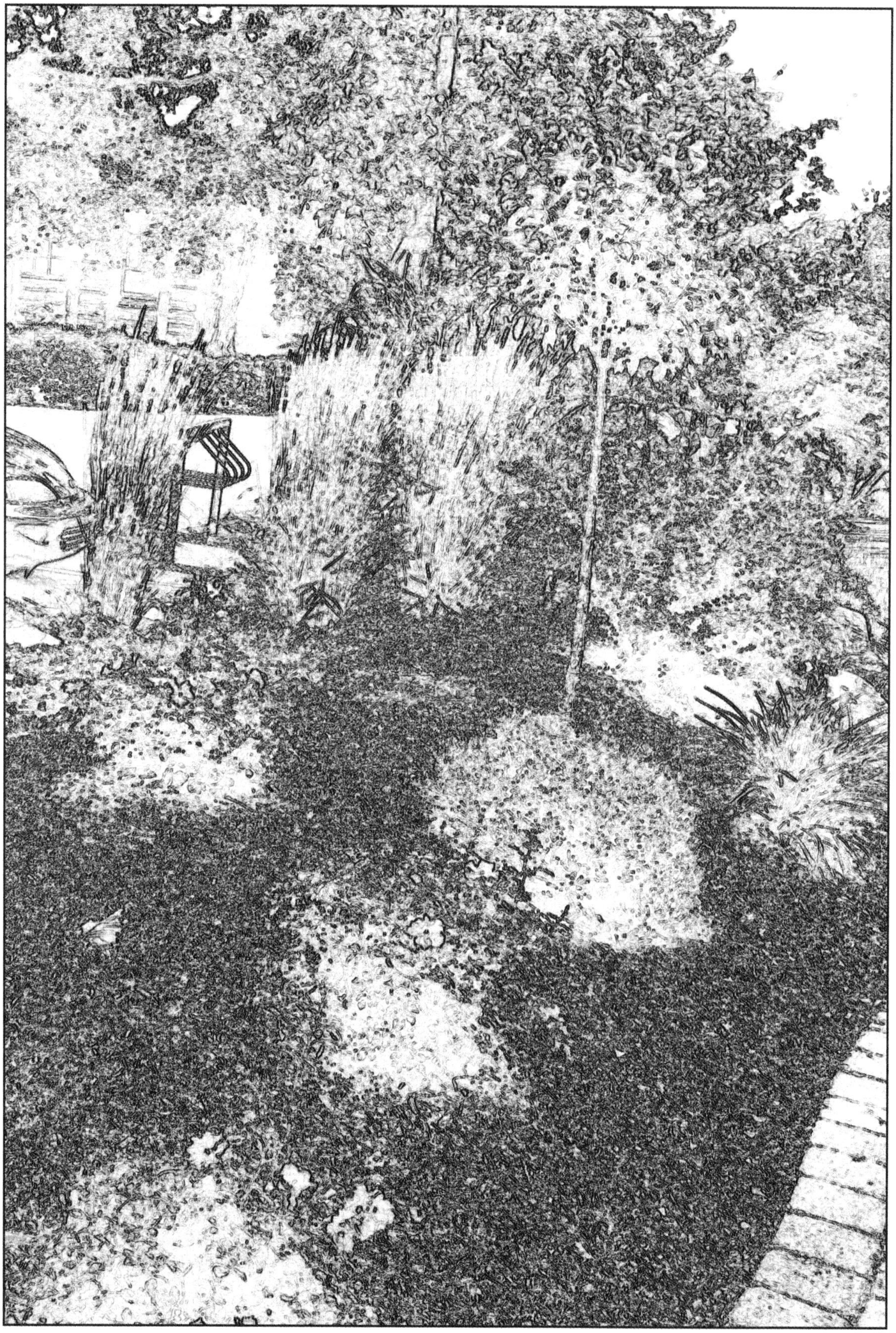

Balance

As with interior design, the principle of balance applies to landscape design. In order for a landscape area of an outdoor space to be balanced, it is important to weigh one side of the planted area against the other side. Refer to the following illustration of landscape plantings around a patio. Plant choices in this plan may be exact repeats from side to side to produce a very symmetrical placement. However, they do not have to mirror each other, but plants of similar height and visual weight can be played off against each other to keep the design from appearing lop-sided.

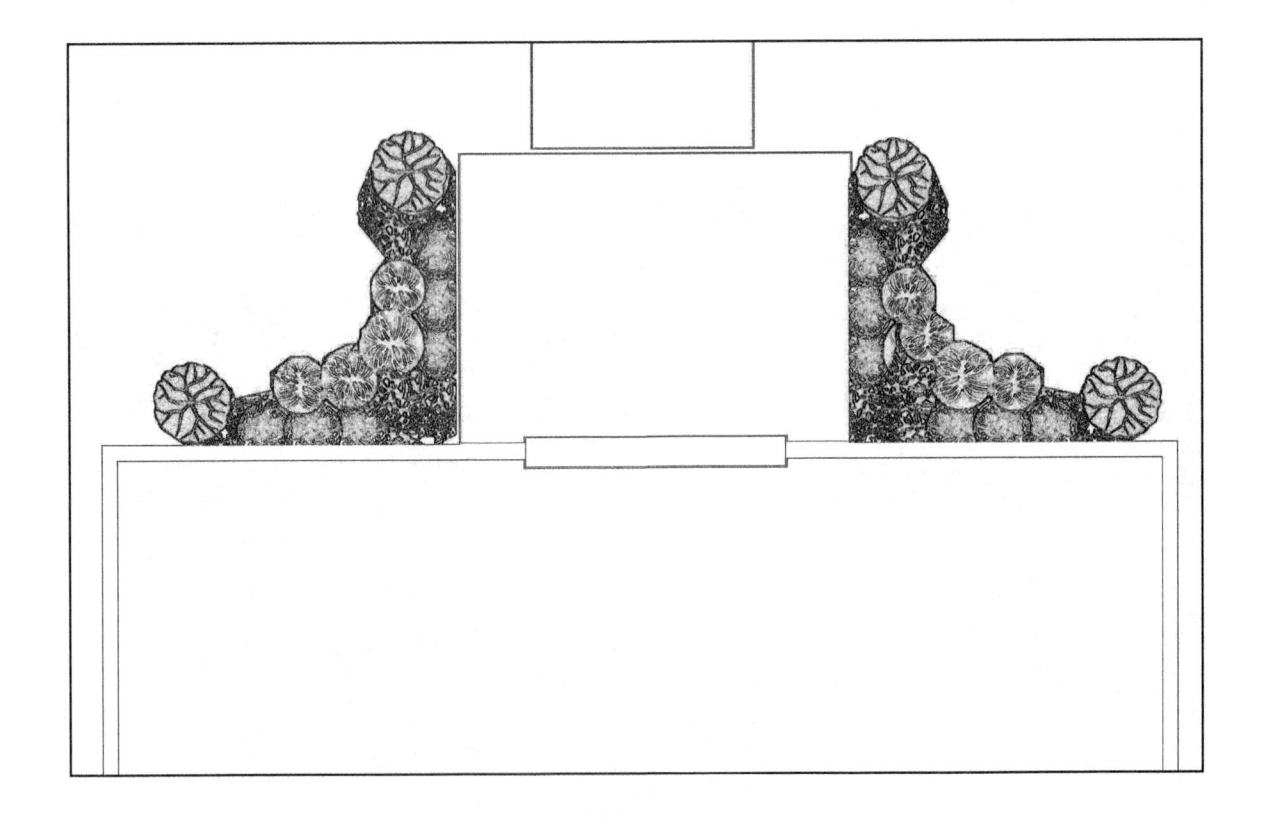

Balancing A Tree

A large tree planted within the garden scheme will become a focal point since it is the tallest plant in the garden. When placing it, it is important to keep it in balance with the rest of the plantings. Although the eye is drawn to it because of its height, plantings at its base work together to support its height.

The following illustration will help you to understand how plantings of differing heights work to ground a large tree in a planting be.

Referring to Fig. 1, the tree marked "A" is planted in the center of the bed as the focal point of the garden. At its base, and extending outward, are lower-growing shrubs and then perennials. The plantings step down in size from the tallest in the middle, to mid-sized, to lowest growing. This arrangement of plantings is rhythmic in that it creates a sense of movement from one height to the next adding interest to the garden. It also works to keep the garden design balanced.

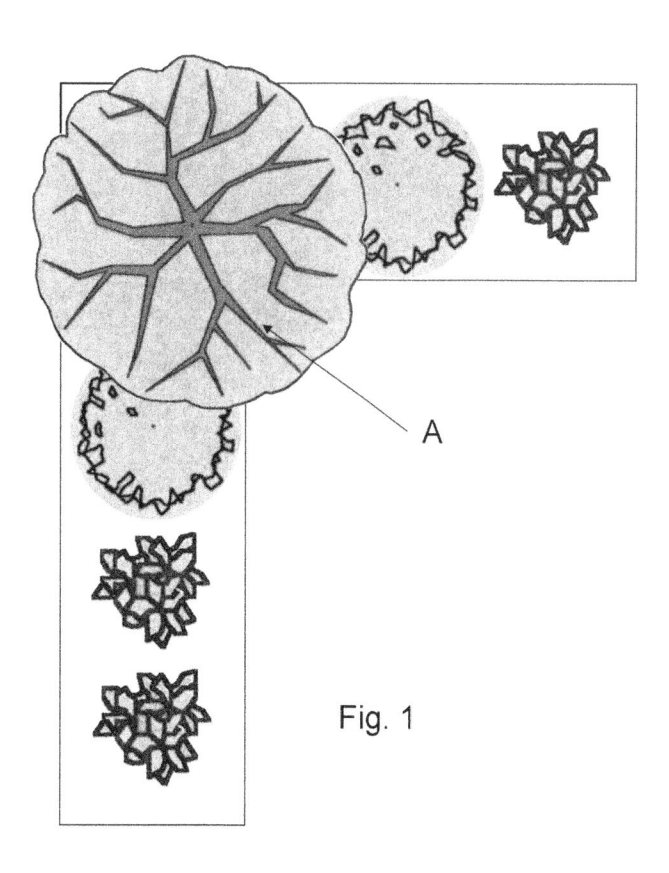

Fig. 1

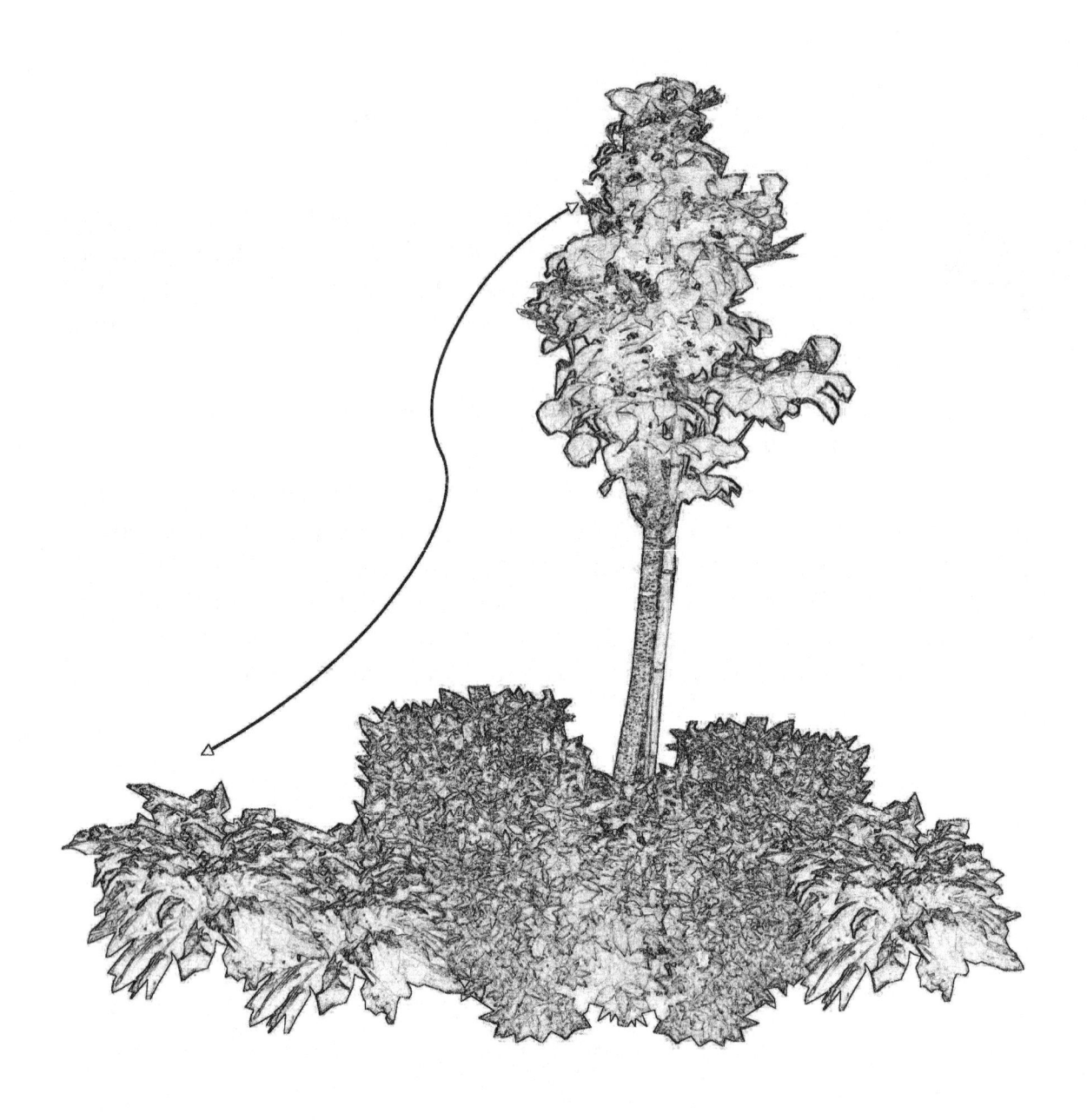

Consider the placement of trees in the following illustrations. Plan A appears more balanced than Plan B. Why? The tree in Plan A is worked more gradually into the plan amongst lower-growing plantings than the tree in Plan B. The design of Plan B appears lop-sided.

Plan A

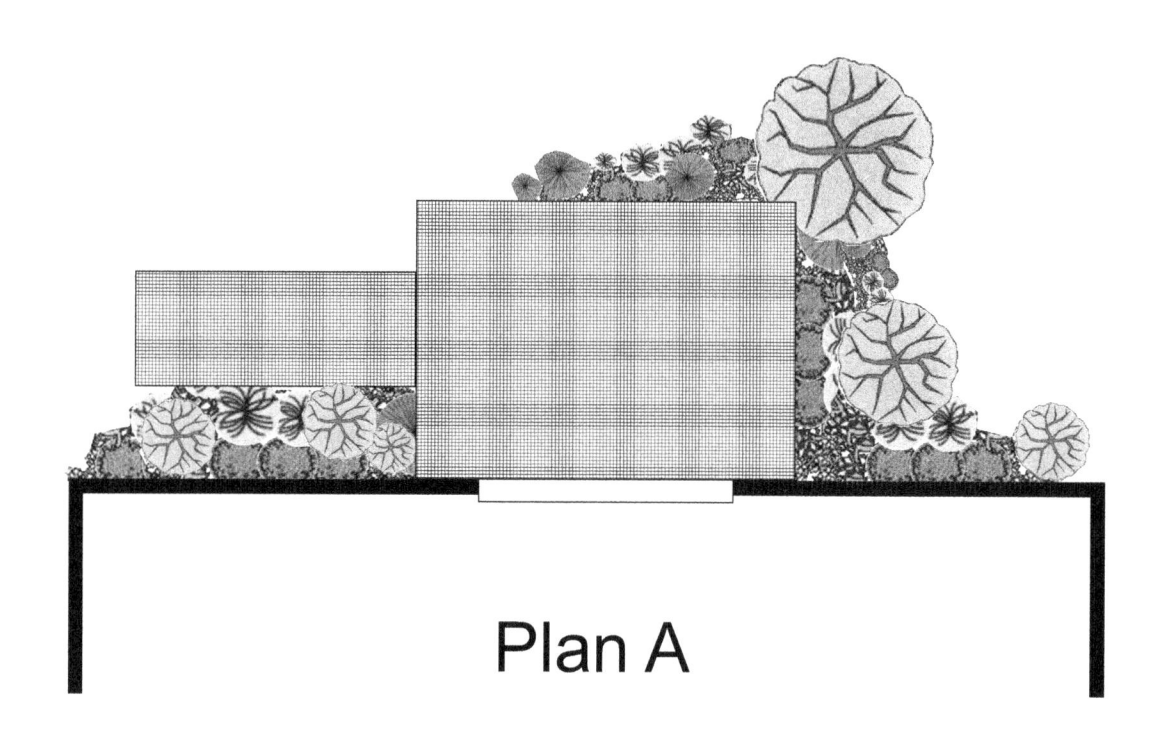

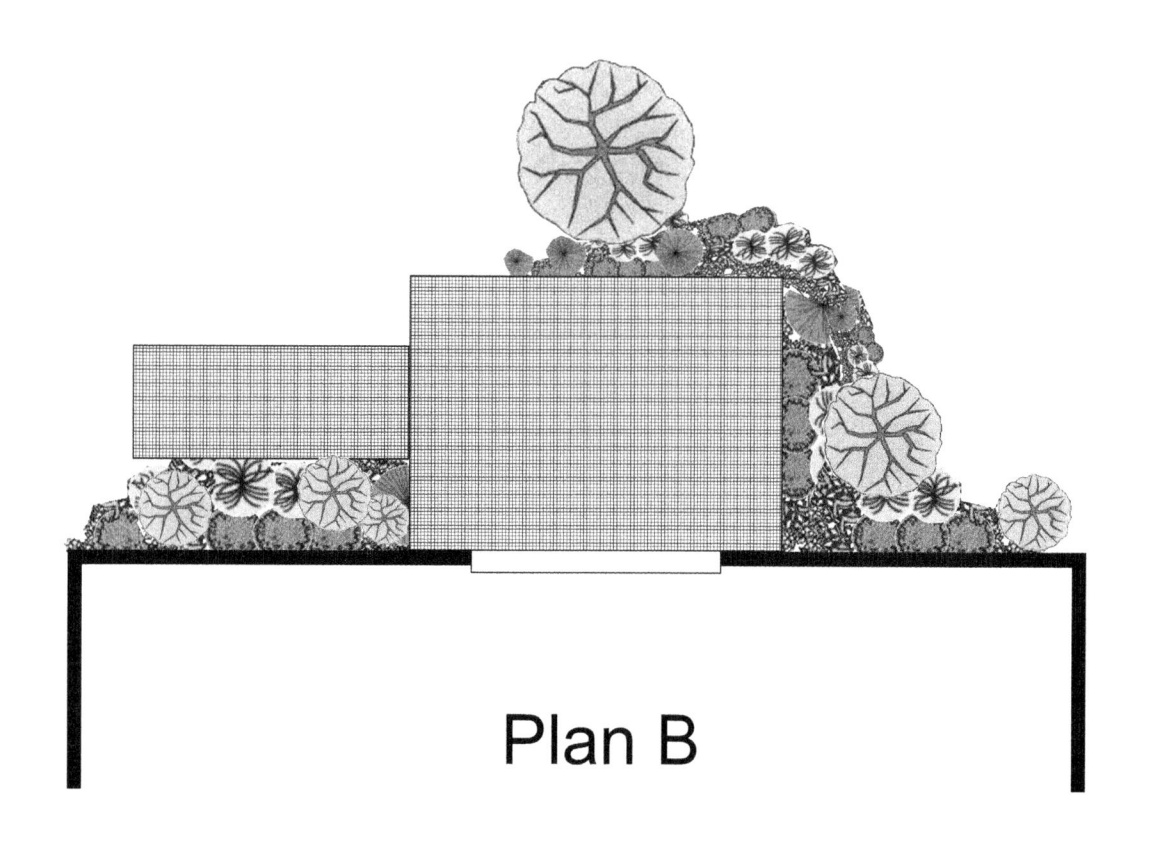

Plan B

Good Proportion

The use of trees can be implemented into a foundation planting that enhances the focal point of the home which is the entryway. Tall trees are planted to the outward corners of the home and plantings of graduated heights, including shrubs and perennials, step down, leading the eye toward the entry. In the following illustration, a vine is planted beside the front door to visually lessen the height of the second storey and frame the entrance, enhancing it as the center of attention.

Note that the full-grown height of the trees is in proportion to the scale of the home, not too large and overbearing, and not too meagre so as to seem dwarfed. Also note the placement of lower-growing and spreading plantings beneath windows which helps continue uninterrupted flow from one garden to the next, but without blocking the view. Shrubs chosen for this purpose are those which will either need to be clipped to keep growth in check, a spreading variety that needs no such maintenance, or lower-mounding perennials. Good choices of shrubs are cotoneaster or spreading juniper. Good choices of perennials are hostas or weeping medium-height grasses.

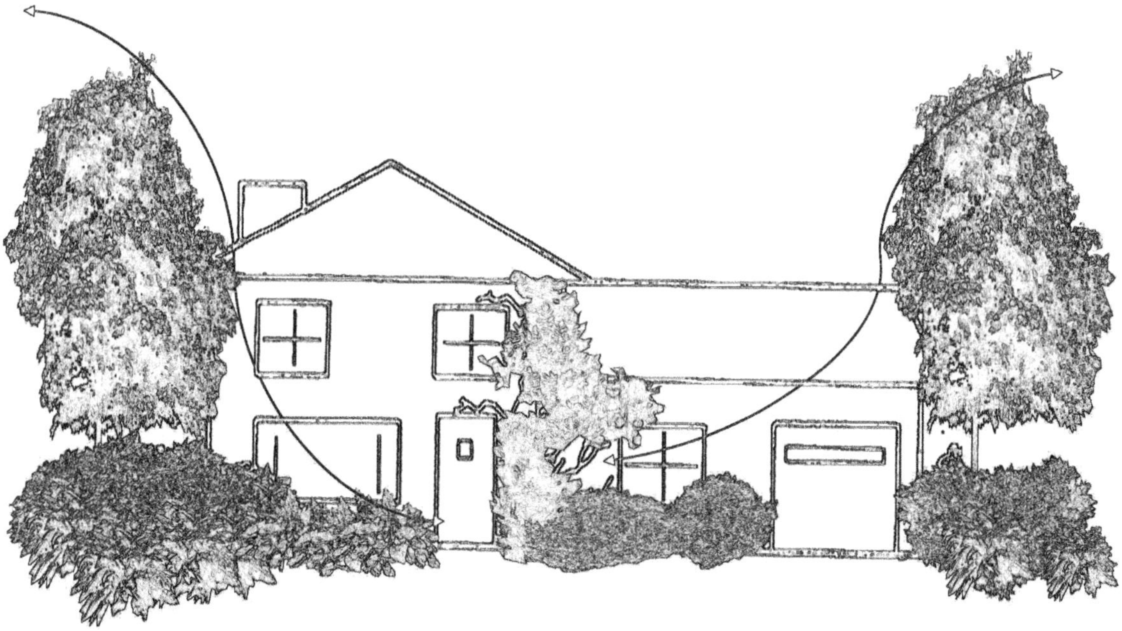

Focal Point

The purpose of a focal point in a landscaped outdoor space is to draw attention at first glace before the eye continues to take in the rest of the scenery. It can be created with a specialty item in the form of a unique tree, a man-made item such as a statue, fountain, or decorative gateway, or any other eye-catching object that is outstanding in the scheme. Because there is only one focal point to a view of an outdoor area, other features are of less significance and are placed in the scheme to help with the flow toward the focal point.

As we have already mentioned, the front door is the focal point of the public area of a home and all plantings work together to lead the eye toward it. In the back yard a focal point can be created as a "framed in" view. This is most effective facing outward from a back deck toward a build-up display in the corner of a yard . A large tree with a seating area below it , a large piece of garden art or sculpture, a water feature or any other significantly unique feature that catches the eye with interest.

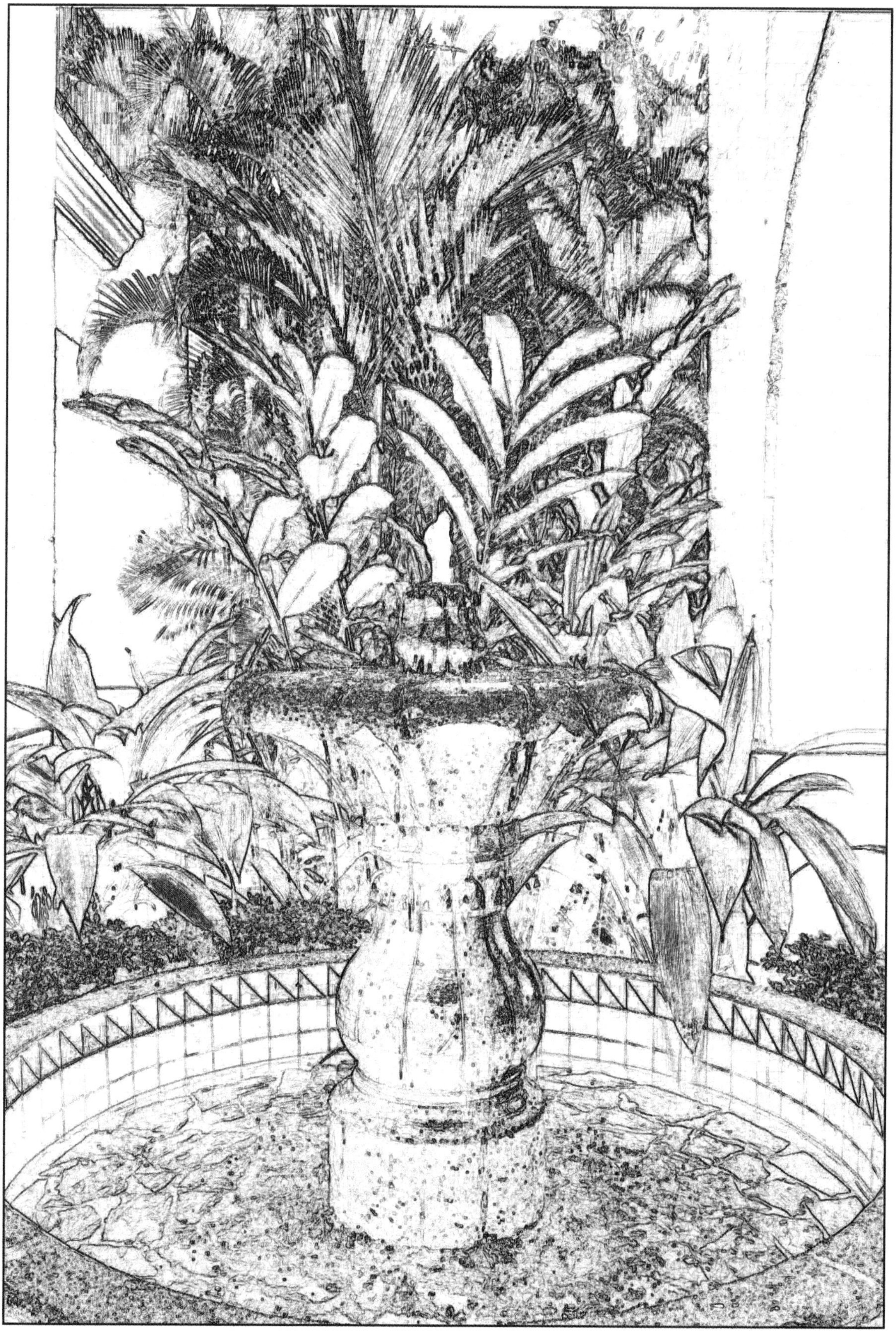

Size & Shape

When designing a garden, the full-grown size, shape, and proportion of plant species one to another must be taken into consideration. Each species has a unique growth form which must be considered when choosing their placement within a planting bed. Some plants grow upward, others bush outward, while others weep in a mound or spread along the ground. Some grow large, others to intermediate height, while others stay dwarfed. They will be placed in the bed to make the best use of their height and form in proportion to those around them.

Varying the heights of plantings in your garden carries the eye up and down the bed creating movement and flow. Mixing upward-growing plants with those that grow outward or weep, such as certain grasses, adds interest to the design while low-spreaders are used to meet specific needs of the bed. Low-spreading shrubs, for example, will be placed in front of basement windows so as not to block incoming light, and ground-hugging annuals will be used to edge planting beds.

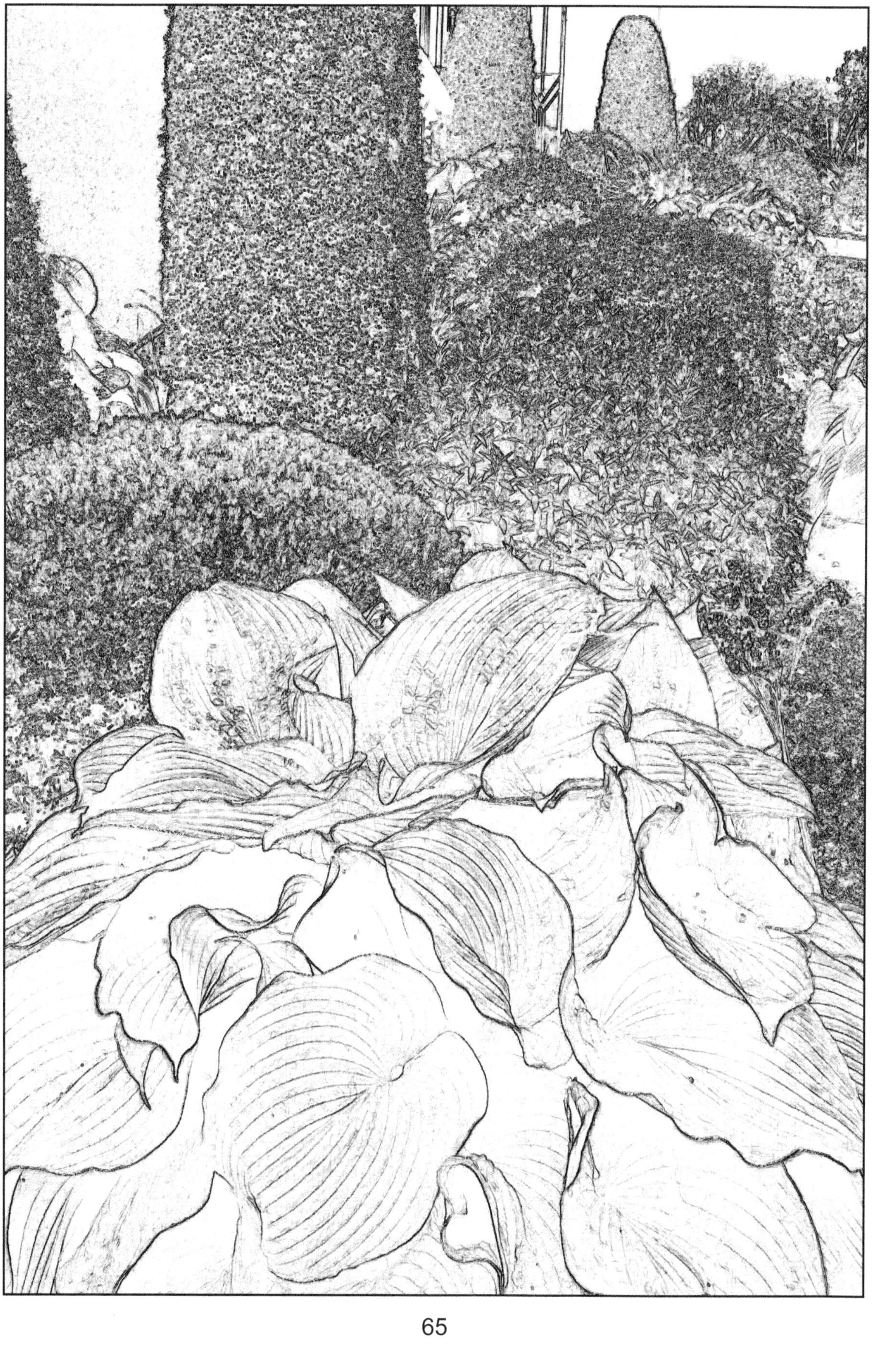

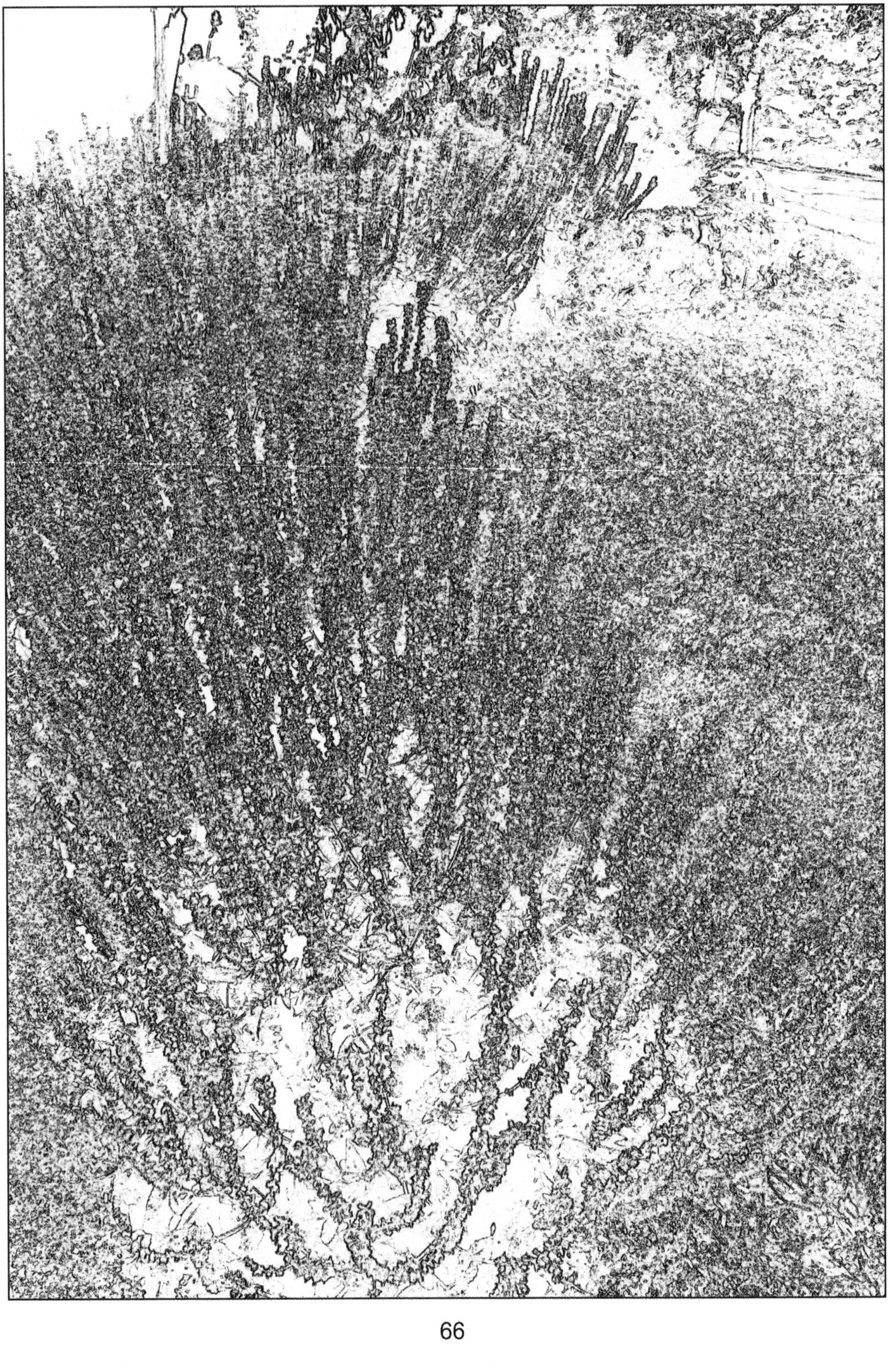

Foliage and Flower Color

The color of flowers and foliage of plantings within the front garden is of importance to designing a garden with uninterrupted flow. Varying tones of green foliage are further complemented with reds and purples, and an endless array of flower colors are available to choose from. Combining these colors in your garden to their best use will prove a successful design.

Soil and Sun Conditions

Not all plants enjoy the same soil and sun conditions. Some grow better in rich loamy soil and full sun while others prefer a wetter environment and shade. When choosing specimens from a nursery, read the planting labels for instructions and pick those varieties that best suit your sun and soil conditions.

Combining Size, Shape, Form, and Texture

When designing your garden, you will need to pay special attention to the variety of sizes, shapes, and textures available in plants. Every specimen has its own unique growth habit and will contribute to the uniqueness of your garden design.

You have studied the shapes of trees and the forms of shrubs, now you will learn about the textures of foliage of perennials and grasses as well as those of trees and shrubs. Juxtaposing a variety of textures one against another in a garden creates interest.

The following garden photos will more fully explain how to successfully incorporate plants with varying sizes, shapes, forms, and textures side by side in a garden setting to achieve a work of beauty.

The conical-shaped clipped evergreens in the following garden illustration stand tall and noble as a backdrop and contrast nicely with the sprawling broad leaves of hosta and clipped ball-shaped boxwoods. The loose-leaf pear tree planted in the center of the bed as a specimen tree adds even more dimension of size, shape, form, and texture to the garden.

In the center of the following garden is a lacy-leaf river birch. It is surrounded by contrasting lower-growing plantings of varying heights, shapes, and textures. Planted at its base are weeping grasses, stiff, pointed-leaf Irises, goose-necked loostrife, tall spikey salvia, sprawling ladies mantle, and scallop-leafed coral bells. The needles of a dwarf blue spruce add still more texture as do the slender wispy leaves and bell-shaped flowers of day lilies.

The abundant variation of leaf form and texture and the variety in growth habit of plantings chosen for this garden compliment without overwhelming each other to make this garden design a great success.

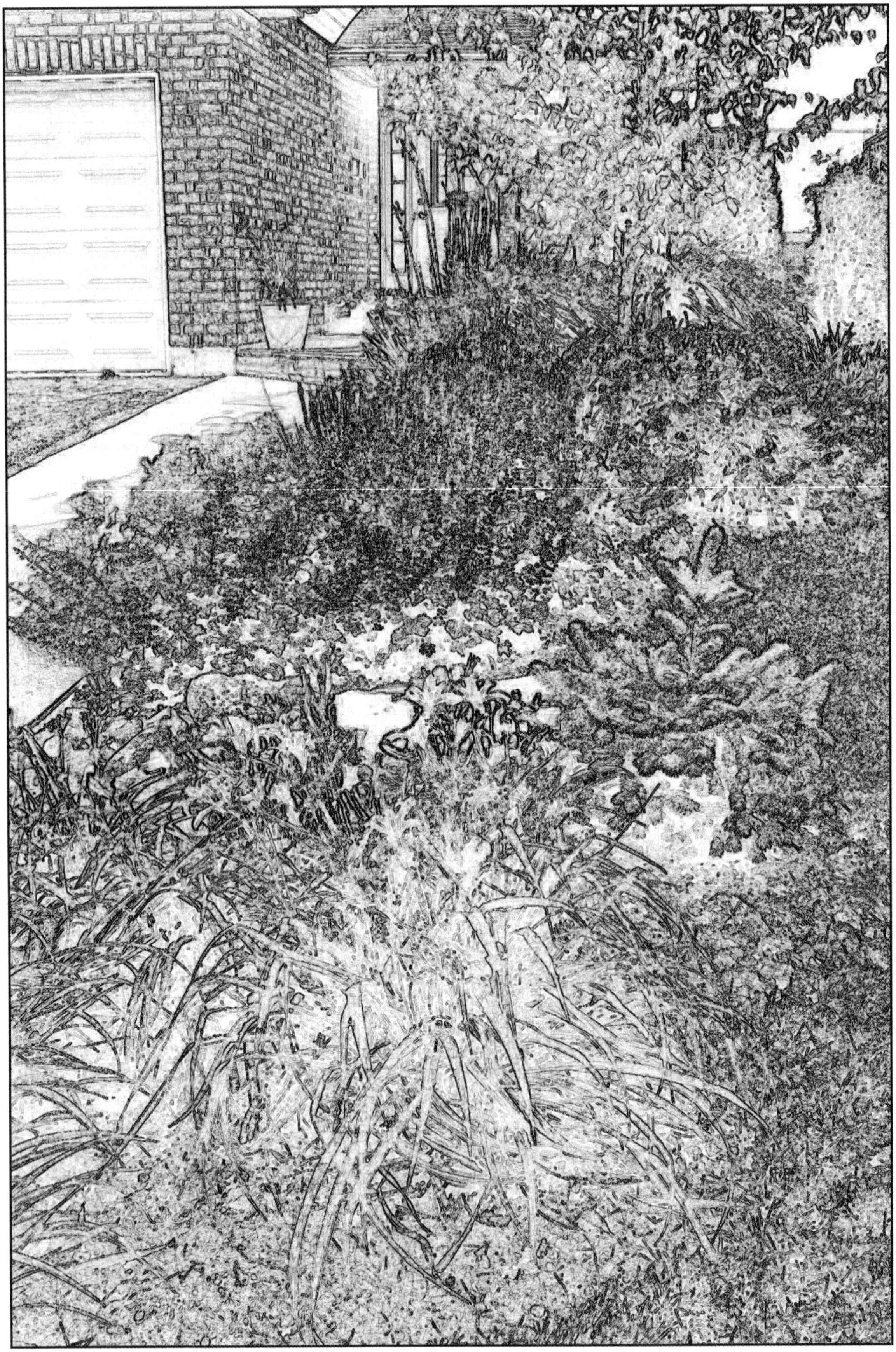

The following garden illustration reveals a combination of giant, broad-leafed hostas, medium scale lacy-leafed potentilla, small clipped and balled boxwood, and spikey daylily backed by a tall conical-formed evergreen. The feel of the evergreen is more formal than the other plantings in this bed, however, don't be afraid to juxtapose formal plantings amongst informal as it brings in the unexpected and adds interest.

Observe, too, that potted annuals have been added to this bed and contribute even more variety in texture and height to the garden.

The feel of this next garden is completely different from that in the above photo. It is more free flowing. What helps to accomplish this are wispy blades of perennial grass combined with the lacy leaves of the Japanese maple. Bushy upright needles of mungo pine and thin blades of Japanese blood grass compliment each other and contribute to the informality of the garden.

Note the varying heights of plantings, from tall to midsize, to small, and then to sprawling. Such variety, when placed in proper order, produces a pleasing sight.

Combining Color

You have already learned that all trees, shrubs, perennials, and annuals add color to the garden, so with every plant added, opportunity is given for more interest.

Flowers alone provide abundant color. Fragrant spring-time blossoms of trees as well as the flowers of shrubs, perennials, and annuals are enough to entice, however, not only do the flowers of a plant add color, but so does the foliage. Even green comes in a multitude of shade variations from pale, bluish-greens, to yellow and orange-greens, to deep, dark, purplish-greens. Added to this array are variegated varieties sporting foliage outlined with white or yellow.

Next are the reds. Trees and shrubs with red foliage take on a completely different look as their leaves turn color from dark to bright red, orange, and then yellow throughout the season. Along with colorful foliage, the trunks and stems of trees and shrubs also add color as well as does their fruit . Especially beautiful are varieties sporting this additional color in the winter when leaves are gone. They make a spectacular display in your garden even in the dead of winter!

Keep the color scheme flowing! Once you have chosen a color scheme for your garden, keep it flowing throughout. When combining plantings in your garden, put effort into combining plantings of differing color side by side for an eye-catching arrangement.

Beds & Borders

Borders are used to line the edges of the property. They are effective when built up against a fenced-in yard or following the line of large trees or as edging along sidewalks and walkways, creating definition between gardens and lawn. Although borders are typically shallower than beds, they can be filled with small trees, shrubs, and flowers arranged aesthetically to provide a colorful flowing display.

To keep boundary lines distinct, borders can be outlined with edging material such as brick, stone, wood, or other materials that can be implemented in a curve to create a meandering line and help more dramatically to separate the garden from the rest of the yard.

Beds can be planted on level ground or raised for height to add contour to the landscape. They can be planted against a backdrop of fencing, a tall wall, or around free standing structures such as a gazebo or storage shed or at the base of a trellis. Beds can add interest to a border when incorporated into it, or for a more dramatic and beautiful view from all sides, be planted independently and positioned strategically within the landscape.

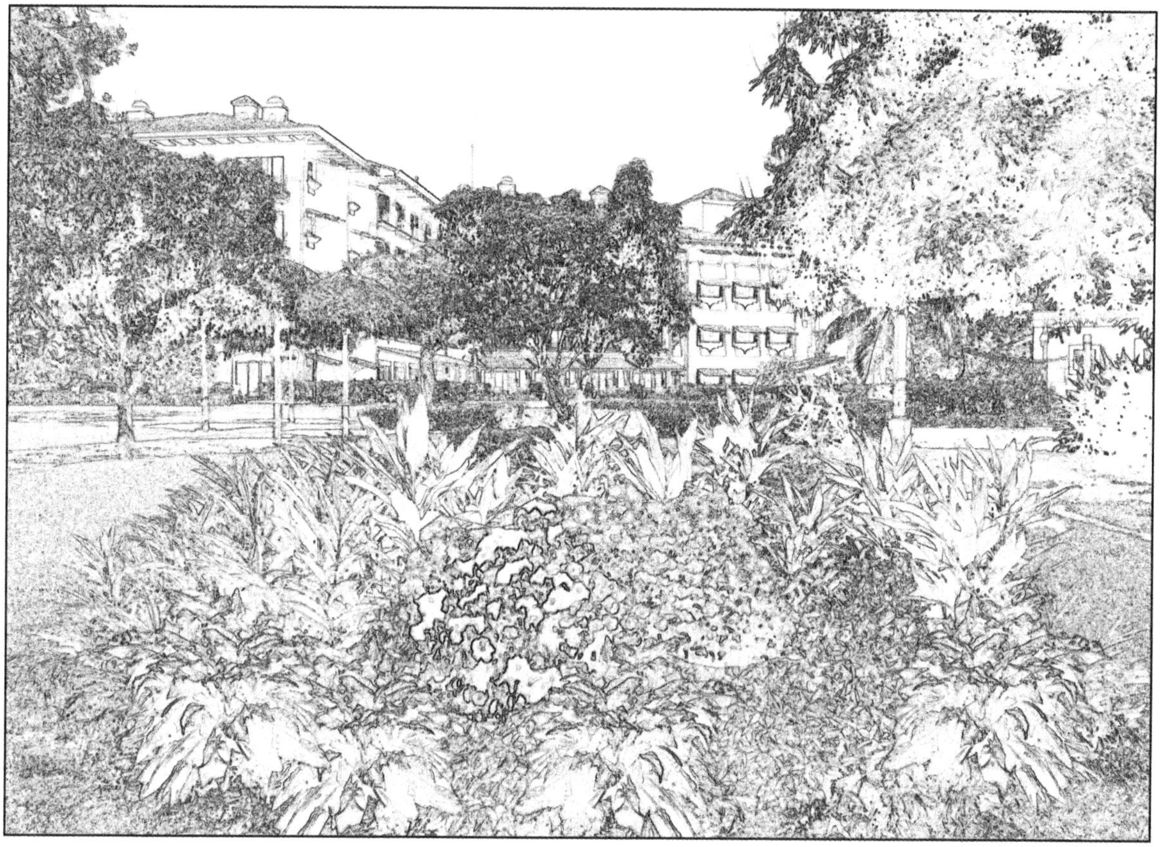

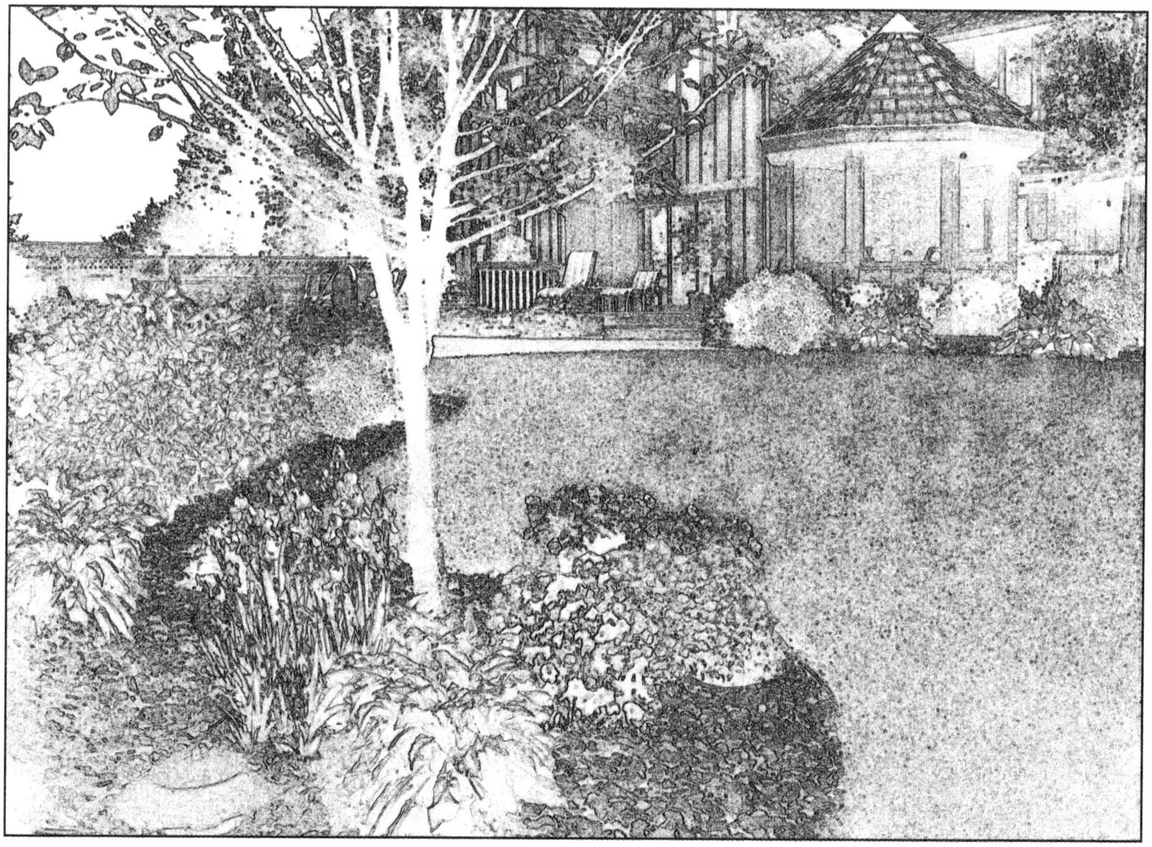

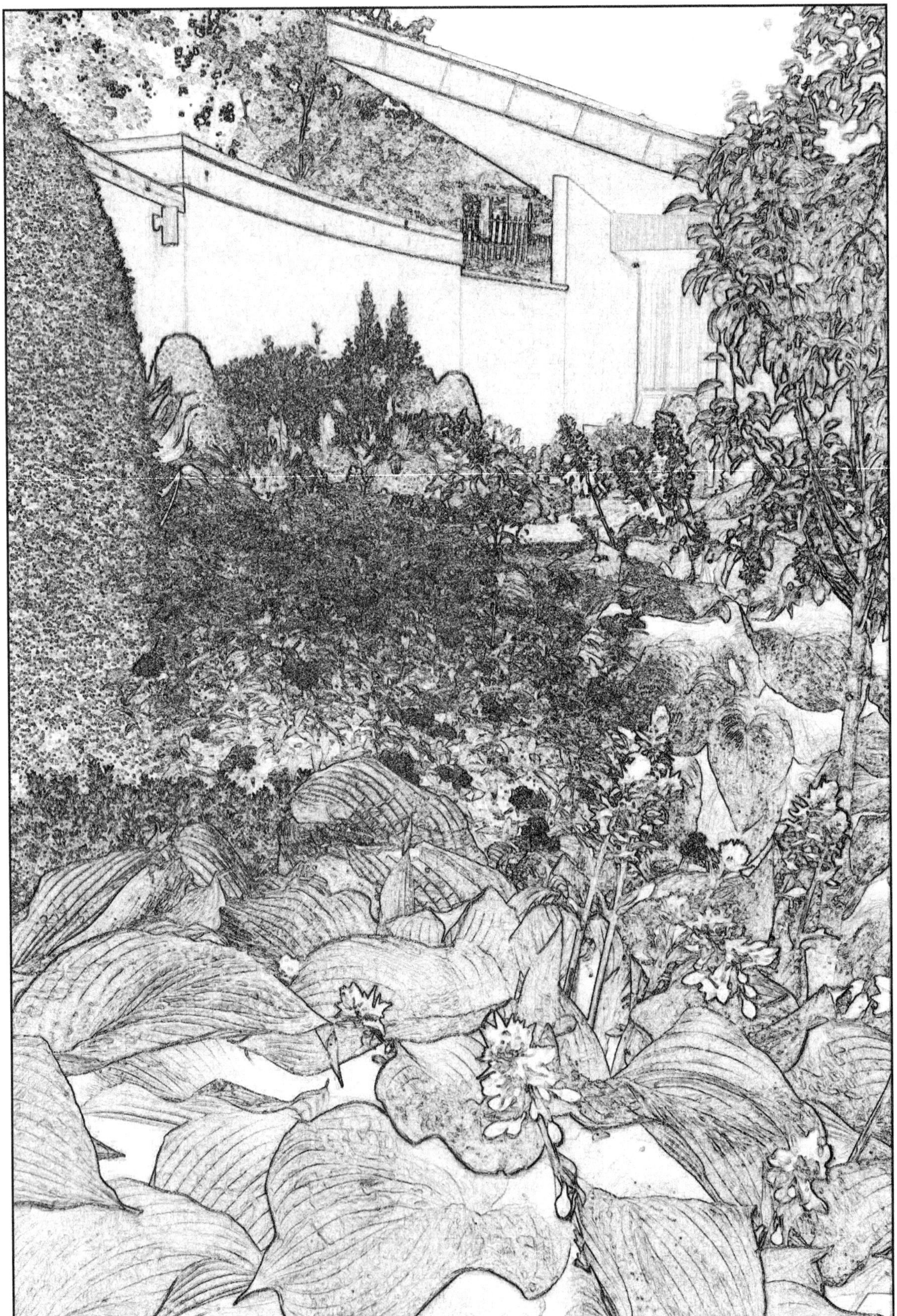

Adding A Garden Bed

Adding a garden bed entails mapping out the area you want to plant into. To shape the bed, use a length of garden hose to outline it. Give the shape a free-flowing edge that compliments its surroundings.

Once you have mapped the bed out, dig the ground up with a shovel, taking a thin layer of earth to remove grass. Dispose of this top layer. Once the top layer has been removed, the remaining soil must be dug up and loosened. These two steps to preparing the planting bed are tedious work and may take several hours, however, if you divide the work up over several days, it will prove less of a challenge.

It is a good idea to improve the soil condition at this point. To do so, purchase and add peat moss. It is also a good idea to add extra top soil to enrich the soil. Both of these products are available from your garden center. The extra bulk of adding these will add height to the bed which will improve drainage. Keep in mind too, that with time, the soil will become more compact as it settles and will lose some of its height.

When ready to plant into your prepared bed, you can purchase potted plants from your local nursery or garden center according to your design plan and follow planting instructions. Once planted, cover the ground around the plants with mulch.

Although at first the bed made seem rather sparse, after several seasons of growth it will begin to fill in. The following illustrations show the progression of a planted bed from one season to the next and how effectively it fills in over time.

BEFORE

AFTER

AFTER

AFTER

Adding Ground Cover

It is recommended that every planting bed be covered with a ground cover to keep down weeds as well as to keep in moisture.

One form of ground cover that is most common is mulch. Mulch comes in a variety of colors and textures and can be purchased bagged or in bulk from your local nursery or garden center. Another popular addition to garden beds has been and continues to be the use of stone and rock to give a more creative approach to ground cover.

Still another type of ground cover is planted. A variety of low-growing plants, including annuals, perennials, deciduous and evergreen, can be used as ground cover. Among them are Artemisia, bishop's weed, ajuga, pachysandra, and ivies. Larger varieties of evergreen include cotoneaster and sprawling juniper. If a lot is sloped, a larger evergreen variety will help to prevent erosion.

Still another option exists; to use flowering annuals as ground cover, massing them along edges of planting beds.

A rule of thumb is to keep ground covers consistent throughout beds. However, this does not mean that the gardener is restricted to using only one form of ground cover in all gardens. Mixing mulch, stone, and rock into the landscape, as well as planted ground cover works to produce unified gardens. Study the following photos to learn how to design with ground cover.

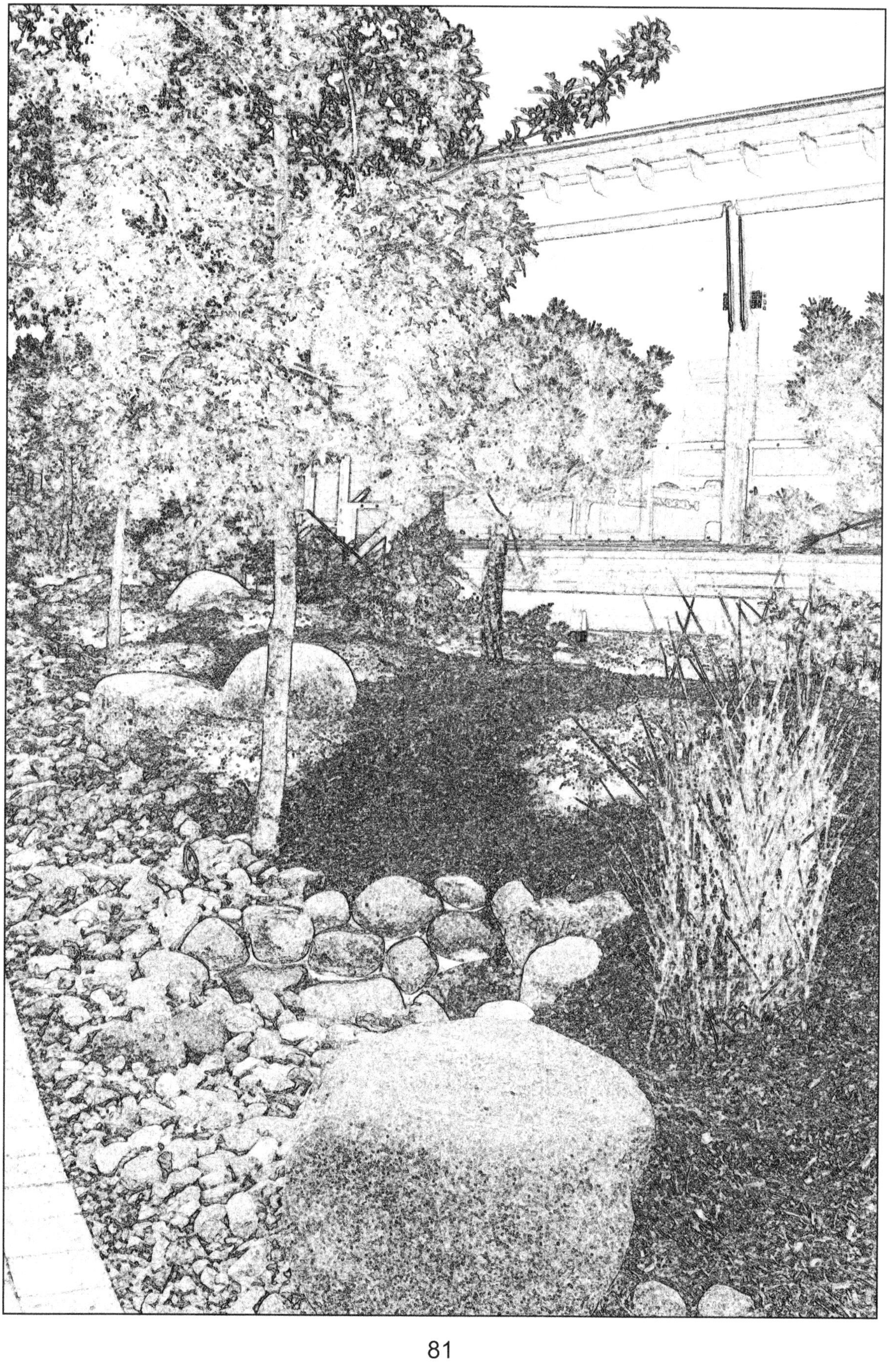

Designing A Walkway

Walkways of varying materials can be incorporated into your garden. Of course we all need a way to get from our driveway to our front door and that answer to that is to build a walkway. This walkway, though fundamental and functional, can contribute nicely to a landscaped front yard. But there are other walkways that can be added to the landscape that are not necessary, but by adding them to the garden setting, add charm and beauty.

Walkways can be included in the landscape as a means of getting from one point to another in the garden, thus becoming a part of the garden itself adding to its aesthetics and lending itself to creative flare. Although this pathway needs to be practical in the sense that it must accommodate walkers, some basic rules apply regarding surface materials and their placement.

For instance, the surface must be safe to walk on with paving material lying flat and secure and pathways although may meander through an overhead canopy of branches, should be kept clear of intruding branches and other debris.

There are many paving materials to choose from when installing a garden walkway including cut stone, crushed stone, brick, wood, wood chip, gravel, mulch, and grass. And these leading through a garden can be surrounded by various mediums as well such as plantings, mulch, stone, and rocks which all work together to create a spectacular garden scene and experience.

If you cannot afford cut stone, settle for interlocking brick, or on an even stricter budget and for a more casual walkway, consider a less expensive and labour-intensive gravel, organic wood chip, or mulch pathway. Not only are these materials more cost effective, but you can save by constructing your walkway yourself and with a lot less restriction in its design.

Begin your pathway by staking out your design. Use a garden hose to mark it out, flexing it till you get the curves and angles you want. Remove the sod and dirt to a depth of three inches and cover with 6mm. clear plastic to assure that no weed can put down roots. If going with pea gravel, use 1/2 Inch stone. To keep crushed stone, gravel, mulch, or wood chips contained, edge your pathway with plastic or metal in-ground border or a decorative brick, stone, or treated wood border. Not only will it keep your pathway neat, it will add to its design.

An additional option for a cost-effective, do-it-yourself version is a loose fitting stepping-stone flagstone garden walkway. This pathway can be constructed in the same manner as the gravel pathway with flagstones laid in amongst the gravel. Alternately, stones can be placed directly within the grass for an even more informal look. Still another option is to forego the plastic underlay, prep with a two inch layer of sand, place stones, fill spaces between stones with soil, and plant ground cover. Good choices are those that do well underfoot such as Brass Buttons, Creeping Thyme, Sedum, Blue Star Creeper, and Creeping Mazus.

If you like the look of a stepping-stone pathway, but prefer a more refined look, incorporate round or square colored and textured pre-cast concrete patio stones into your design. You are not limited. You can put your creative thinking to the test to create a pathway through your garden that suits your style.

Once your pathway is in, add gardens along its length to soften the edges and enhance the beauty of your meandering path. Whether your walkway meanders through an open myriad of trees, shrubs, and perennial gardens, or is restricted to a smaller private setting, it is sure to beckon its viewers to stroll it and more fully appreciate and enjoy its lovely surroundings.

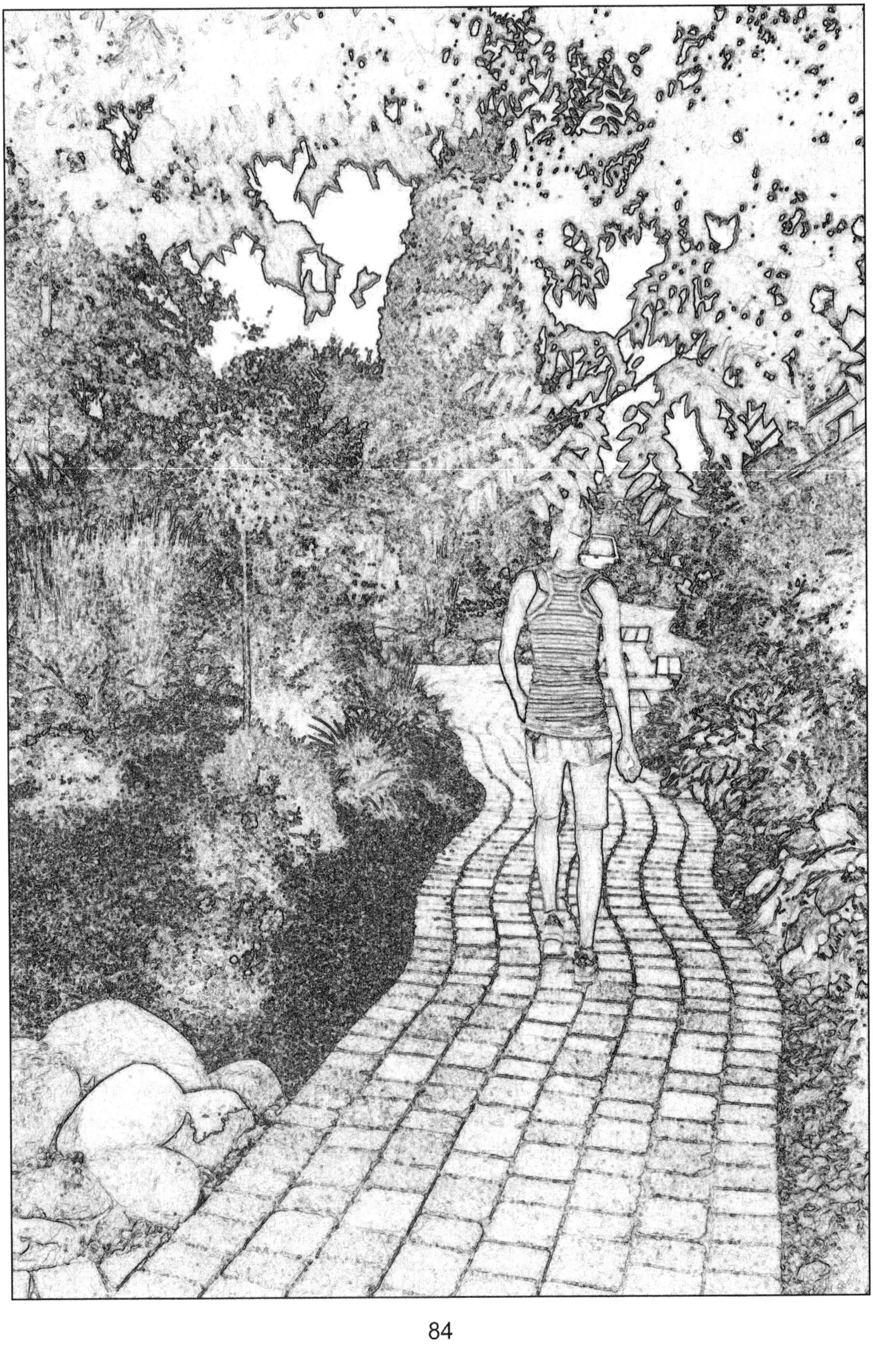

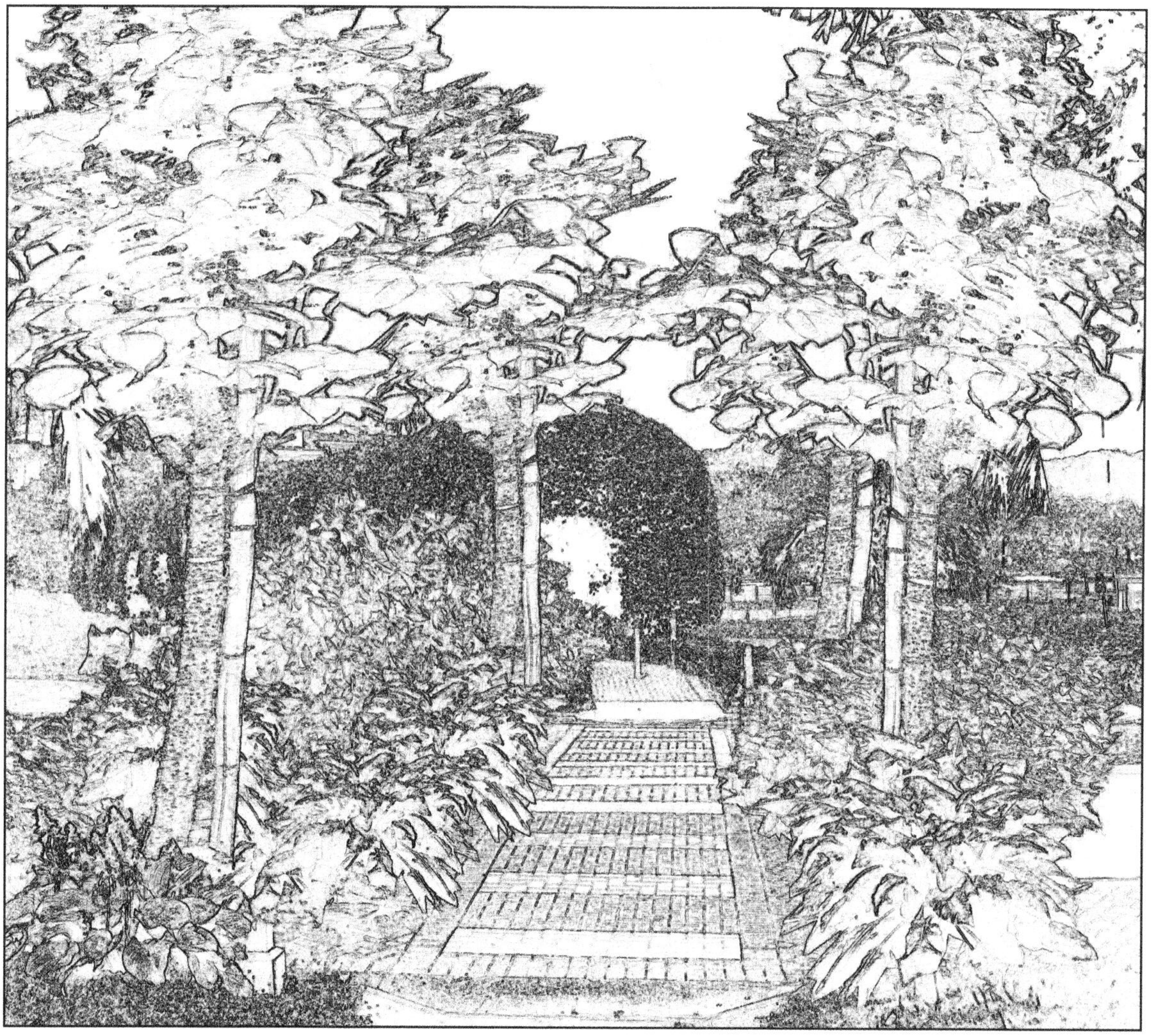

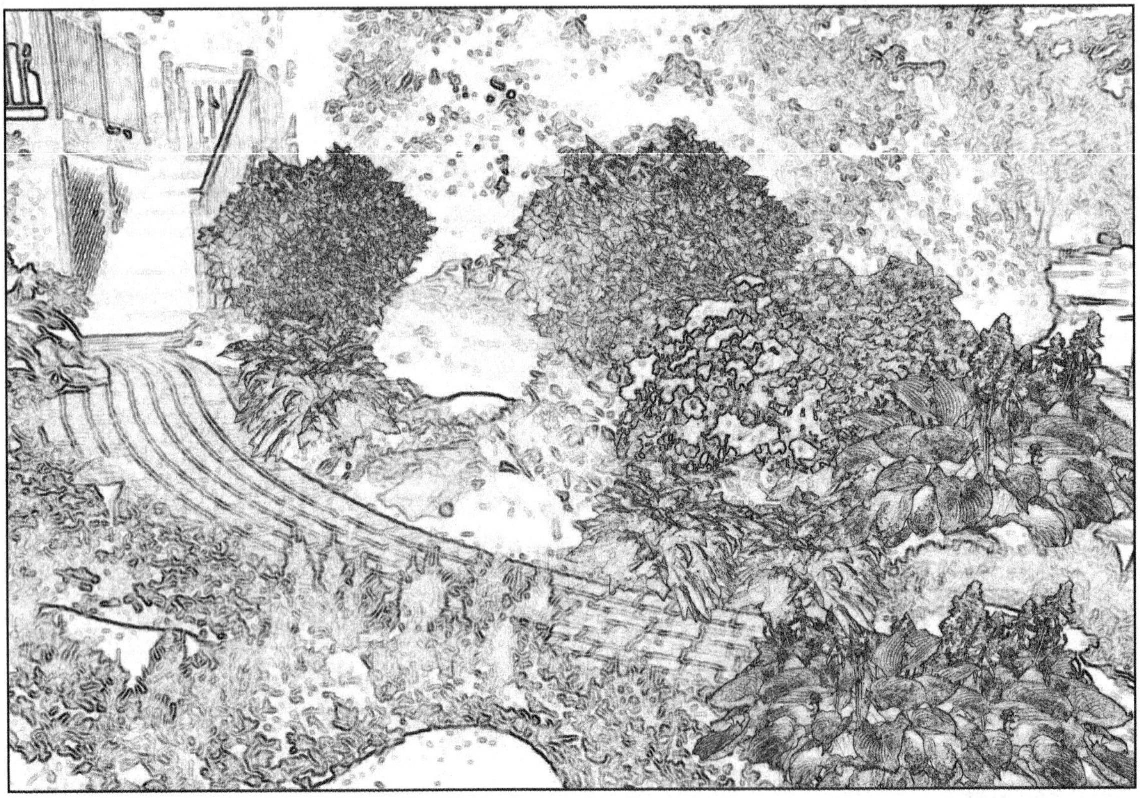

87

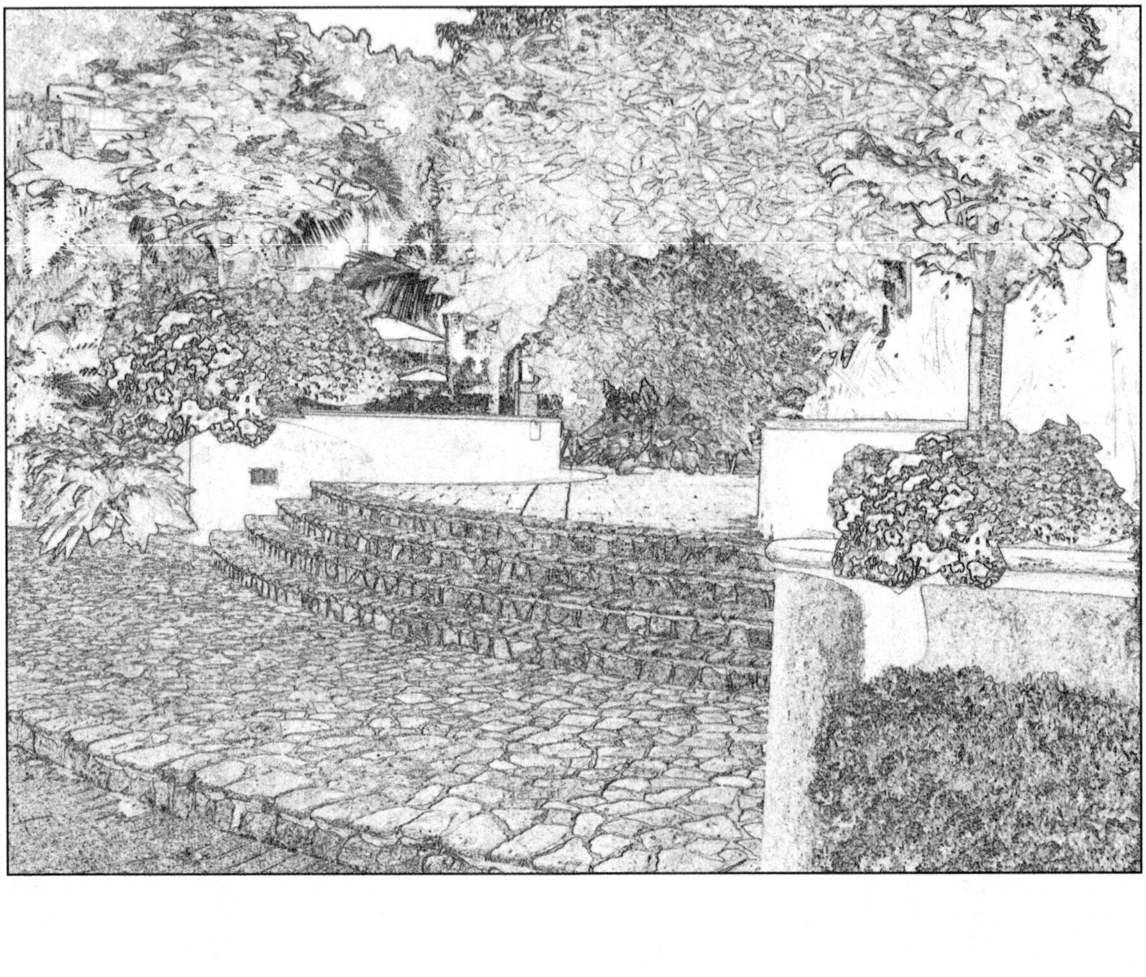

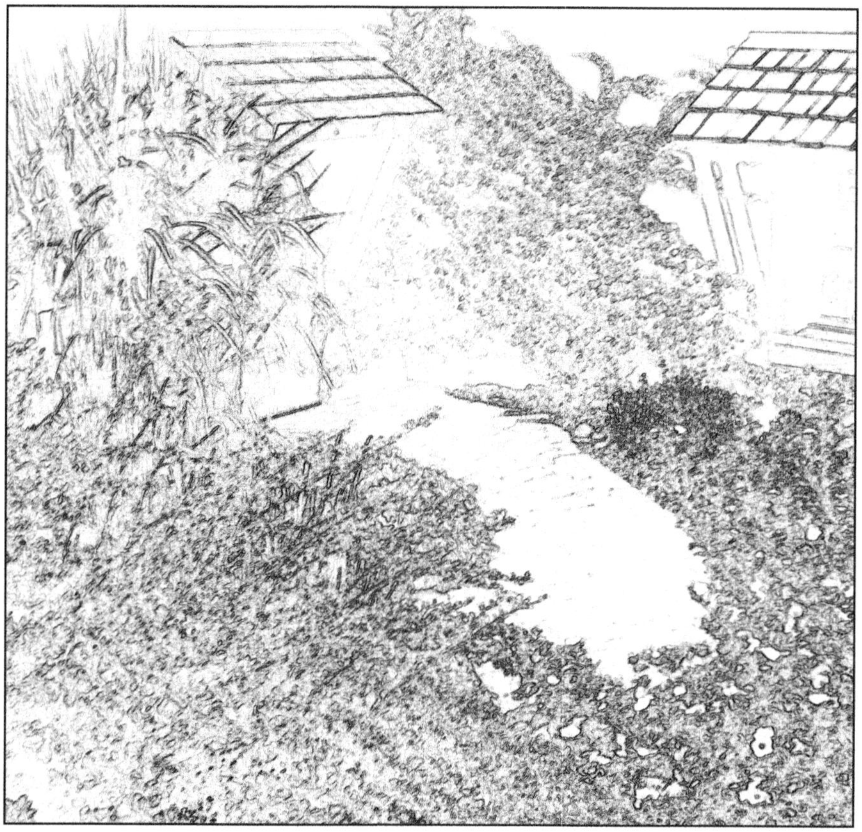

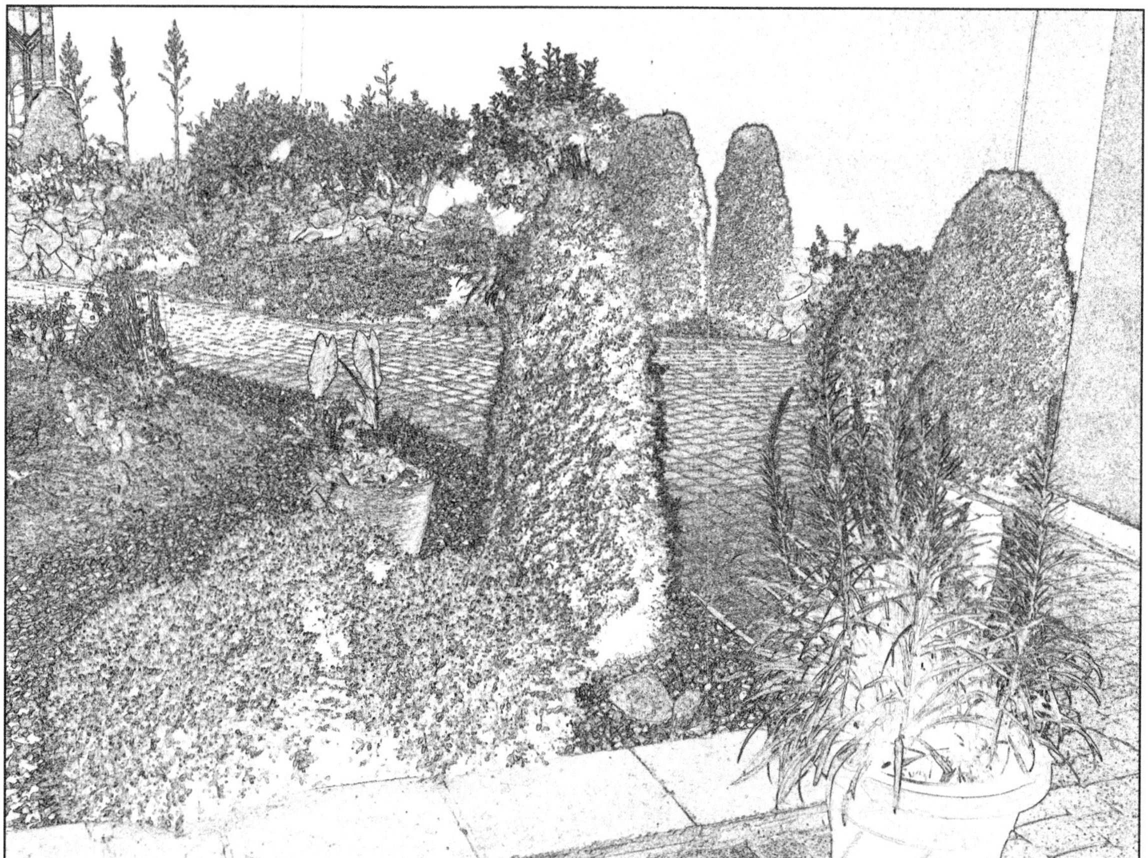

Designing a Walkway with Stone

You may have a front porch and steps down to your yard, but you might lack a walkway leading to the driveway or garage. An easy way to create an informal cottage-style walkway is with slabs of flat stone known as flagstone.

Dig up the area you want to pave, remove the top soil, level the ground and you are ready to build your walkway. To keep weeds from coming up between slabs, lay a piece of 6 ml. thick plastic down before the stone. Keep the surface of rocks level and fill gaps between with stone.

When designing your walkway, wind it around a planting bed that provides a handsome display of perennials.

The following illustration is included to give you an idea of what an informal walkway could look like. For a more formal design, consider paving with interlocking stone.

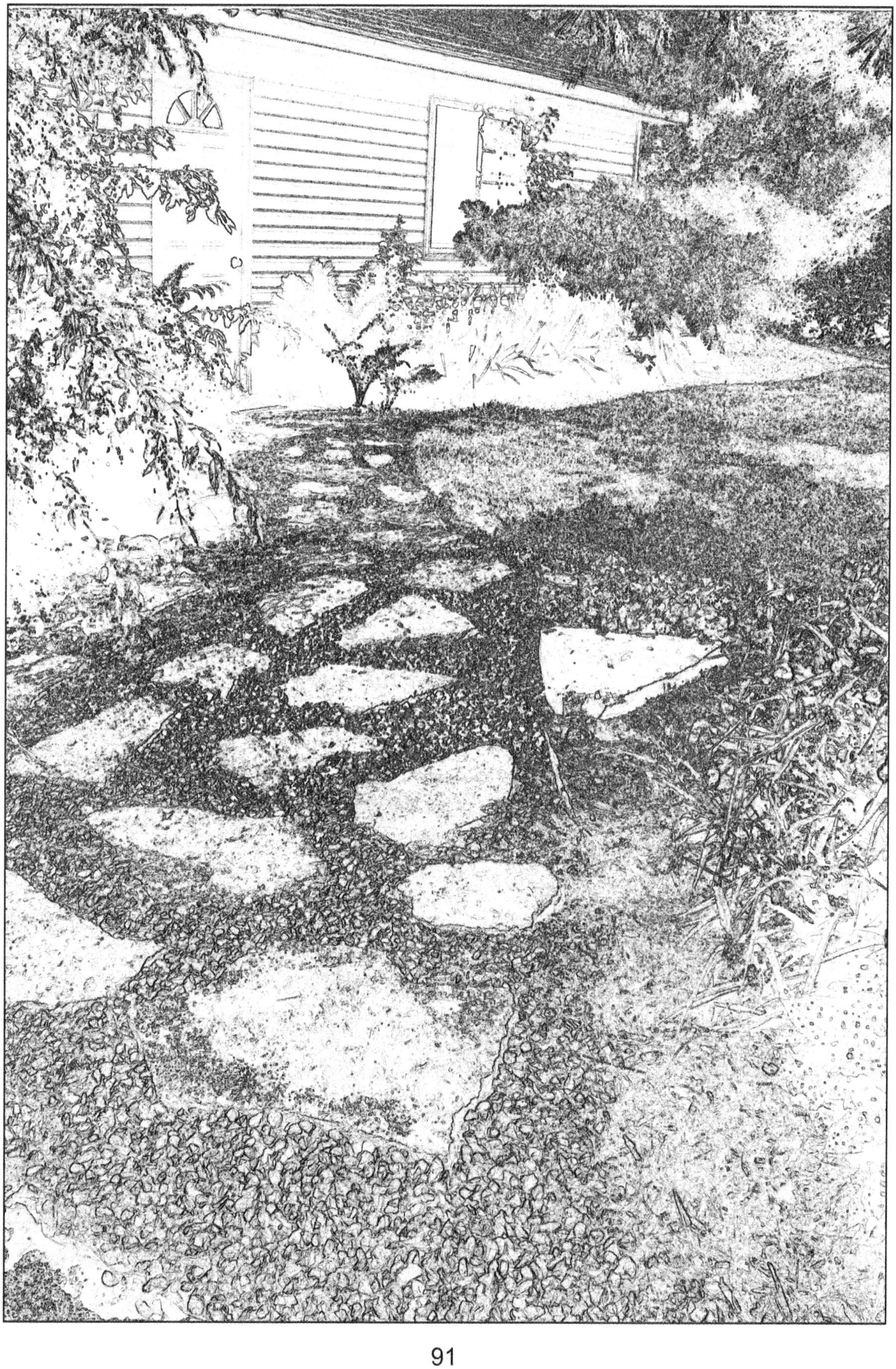

Landscaping On A Slope

When planting on a slope, choose ground-hugging shrubs and intersperse them with trees, perennials, and perennial grasses. Mulch the bed to keep down weeds and to keep watering to a minimum. Add rock for interest. Densely cover the slope or keep plantings sparse. Either way, consider their growth habit and full-grown dimensions prior to planting . If the lot is extremely steep, add large boulders to keep the soil from running off, or where possible, add a retaining wall.

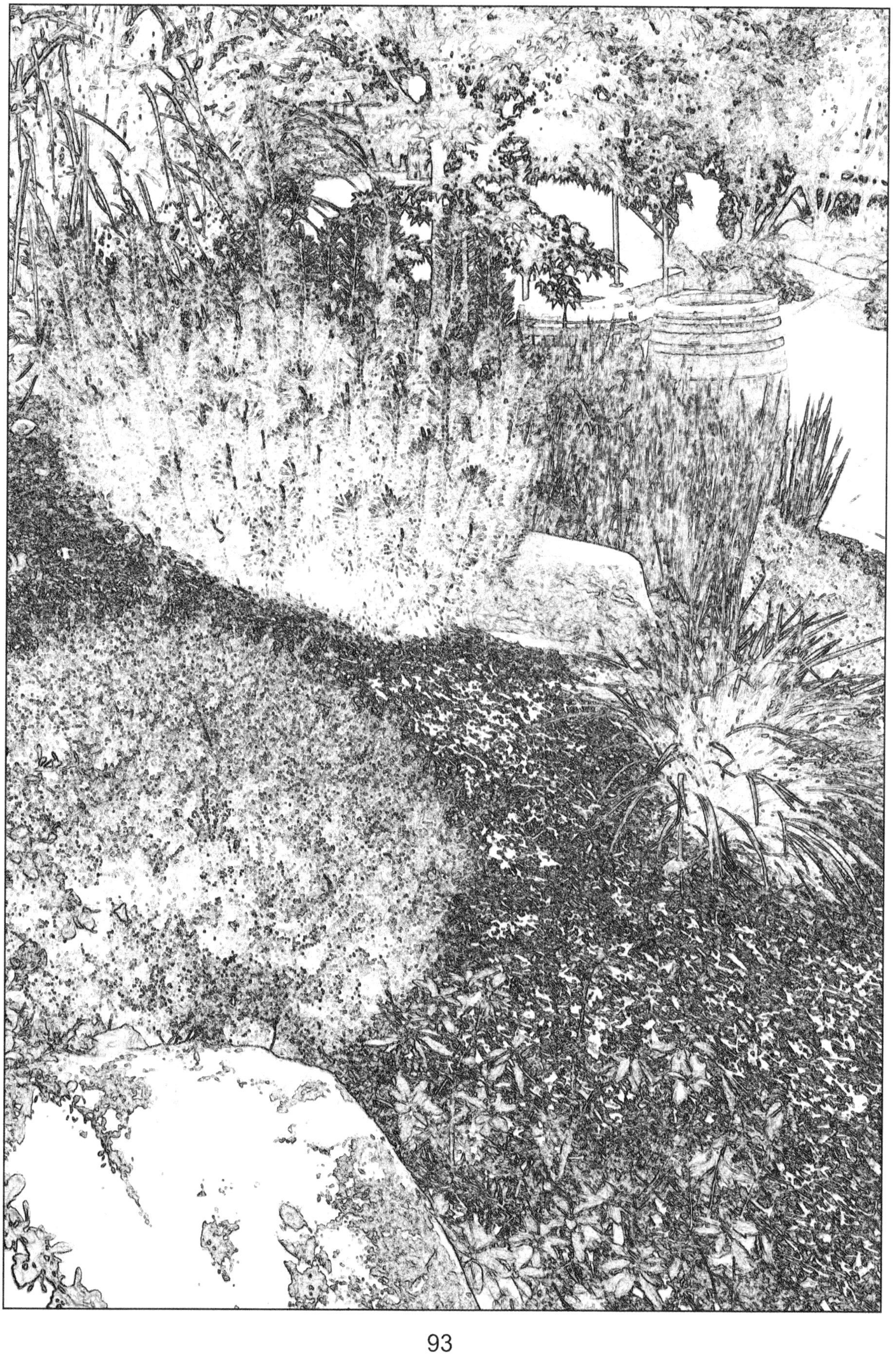

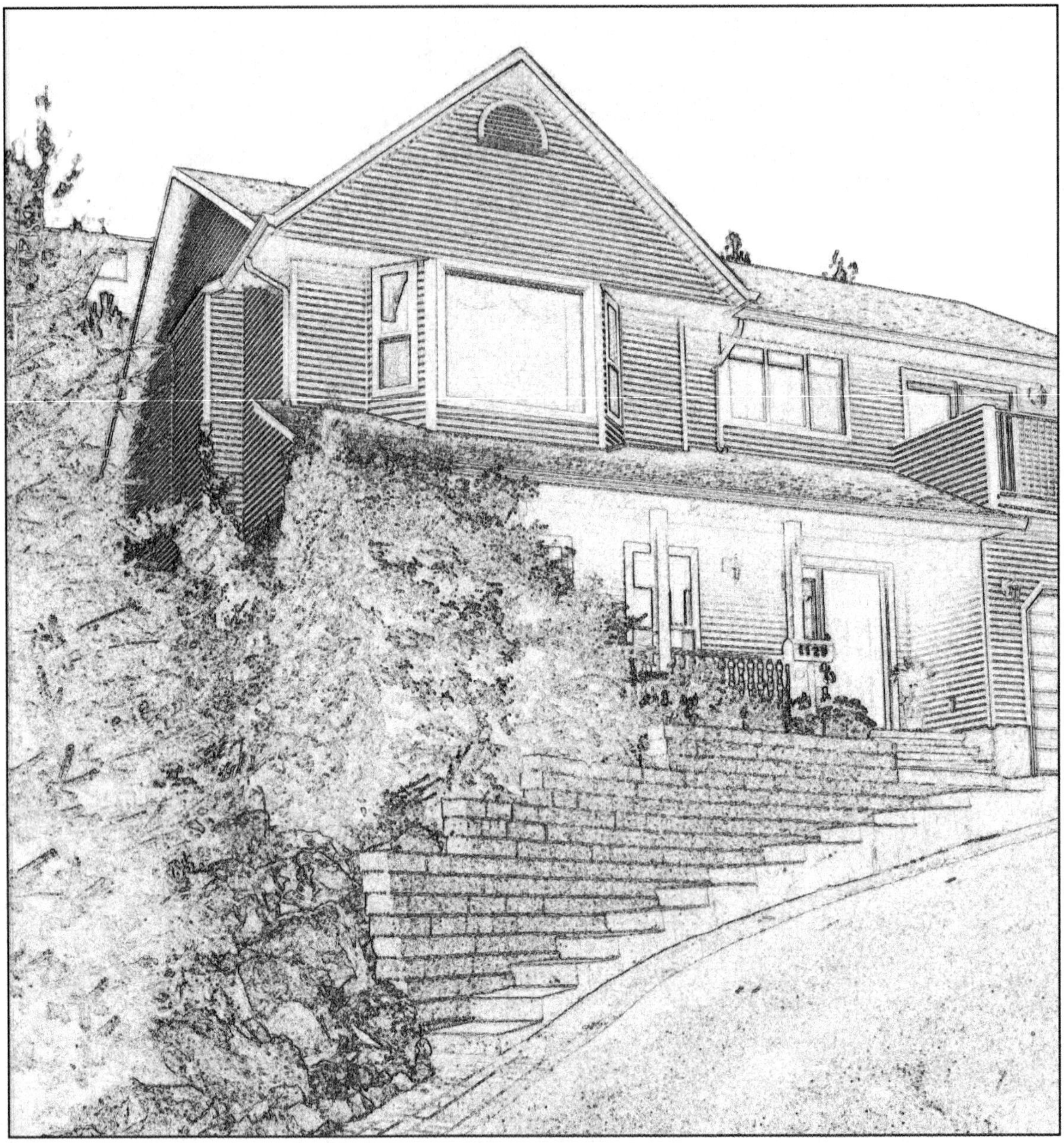

Landscaping with Rock and Stone

Rock is a beautiful addition to almost any garden whether used as a focal point, as a continuous covering providing interesting variations of heights and contours to an otherwise level grade, or as a solution to a dry and rocky terrain or one that is sloped and easily erodes. Another popular use of rock in a garden is to build a dry creek bed to help with drainage.

Although the emphasis of the garden is on trees, shrubs, flowers and ground cover, adding rock to it is a simple, easy way to add to its aesthetics. Natural rock, although hauled in from a distance, will look right at home in any garden. Integrating it into your landscape will quickly add a naturally rustic feel that allows it to easily become a viable part of your garden environment.

For most impact, use large boulders with interesting shapes and angles to build levels into your landscape, holding back soil and acting as a retaining wall, or set them into place in groups of three, four, or five in various sizes and shapes throughout your landscape. Because rock is found naturally in rocky or mountainous environments, put them to use on slopes and incorporate plants native to mountainous areas into your scheme to take advantage of their unique character . Set each rock firmly into the ground, not only to make them appear as though they are a natural part of their surroundings, but also to keep them from rolling downhill.

Smaller sized rocks and stones can be successfully incorporated into the landscape as well as larger rocks and using both compliment each other and add to the sense of belonging as well as drama. Add them in pools throughout the landscape, interjecting them here and there, using them as mulch beneath plants, or completely covering a section of garden with them alone. A good example of such use is in spots in your garden that are too wet or too shady to successfully grow plants. A covering of smaller rock and stone can take the place of plants, keeping continuity in the garden bed and contributing unique character to the landscape design as a whole.

Of course stone, including flagstone and river rock, can also be incorporated into the landscape design by the creation of pathways to and through the garden, borders to edge gardens, along driveways, as well as in garden walls, all of which play off the greenery of garden plants and add still more opportunity for color and textural interest.

Whether you just want a splash of texture to your garden, or need to have find a fix for problem areas, rock and natural stone are a wise choice. They are durable, maintenance free, and add substance, character, and natural impact to your landscape throughout the seasons. Bring them into your scheme in all shapes and sizes to add such unparalleled uniqueness to your garden.

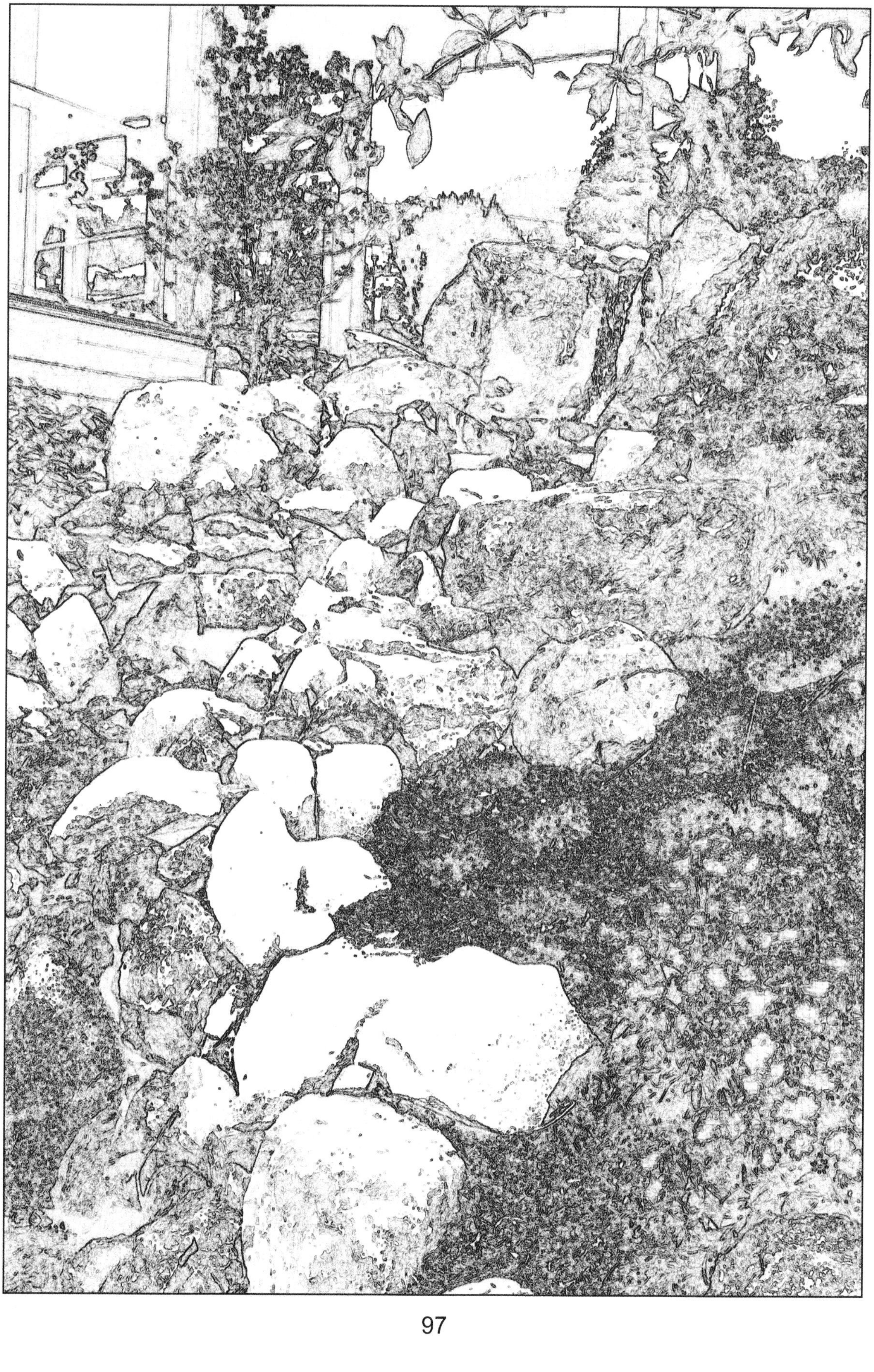

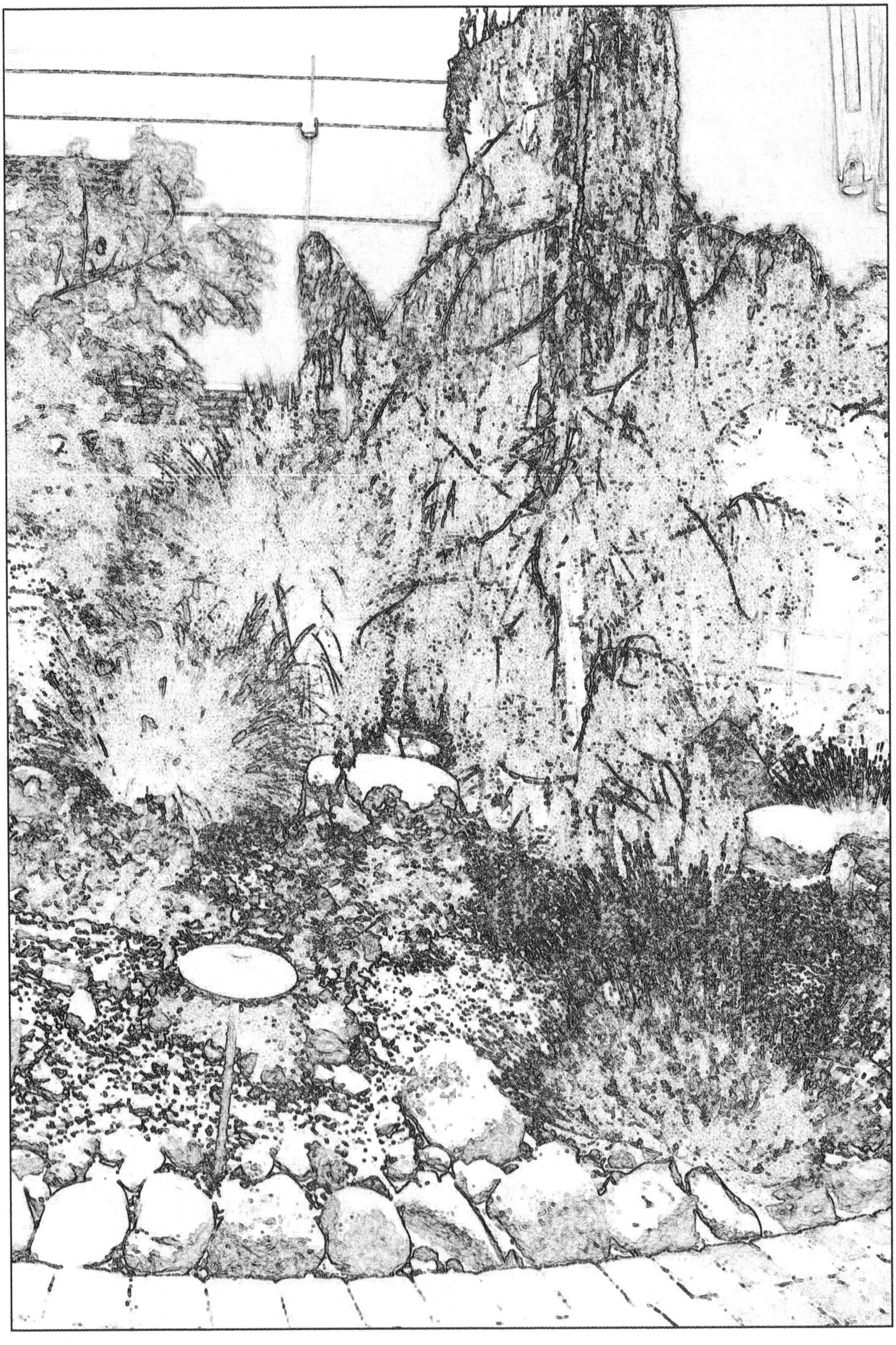

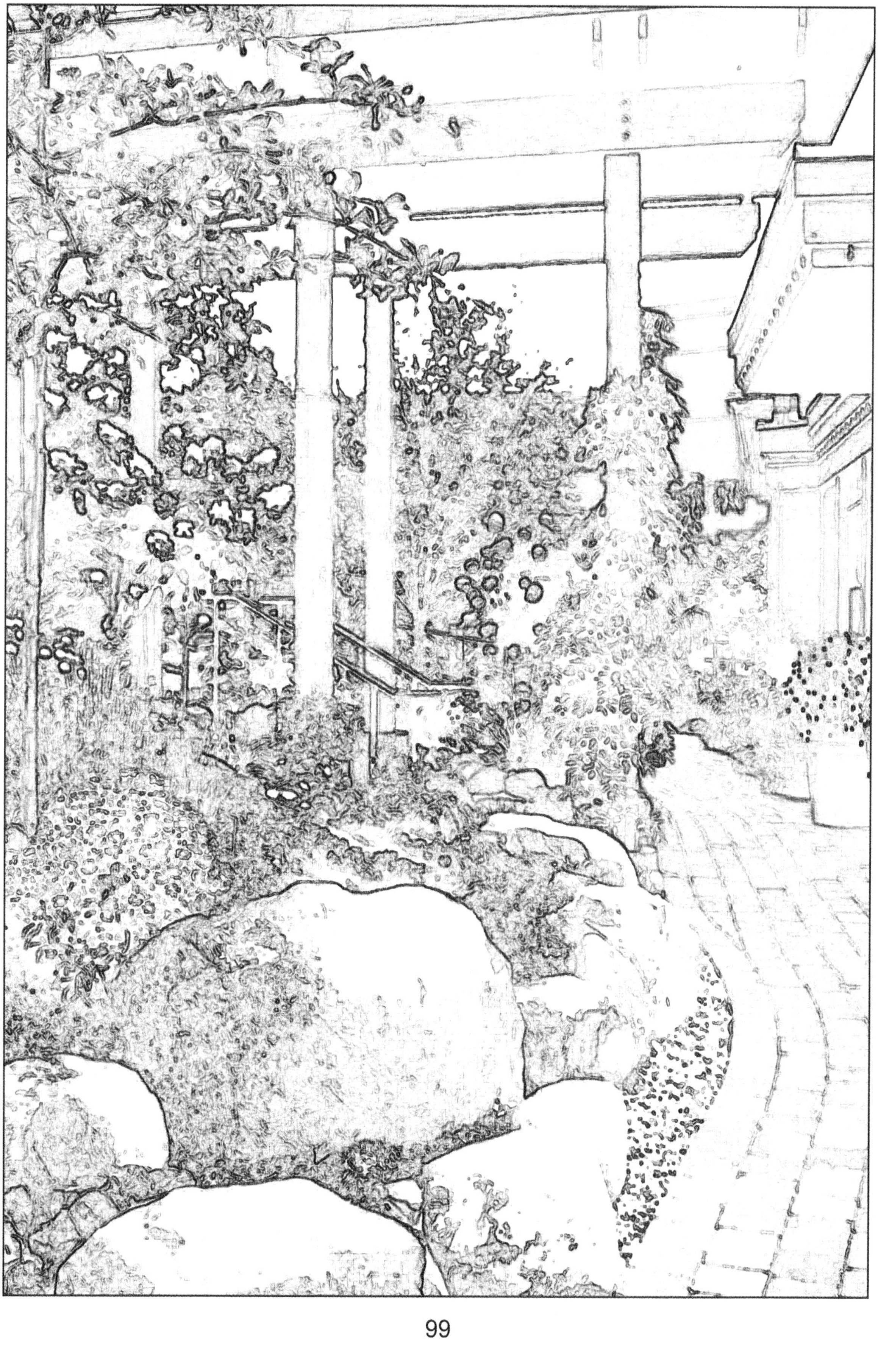

Selecting Trees

Trees come in all shapes and sizes and fall into two categories, deciduous, and evergreen. Deciduous trees have leaves which they lose in the winter. Evergreens, including those known as coniferous trees, bear needles which they keep throughout the winter. The following considerations need to be made when selecting trees for your front yard.

1. The full-growth height, width, and shape
2. The density of the foliage
3. Leaf or needle texture of tree
4. Does the tree change color seasonally?
5. Does it flower or bear fruit?
6. Is the tree zone-hardy

It is important to know the dimensions a tree will be when full grown in order to keep proportion right. A one-storey home will be overwhelmed if trees are proportionally too large and if plantings are too small for a two-storey home, they will looked dwarfed in proportion to the house.

Shape is important too. A dense pyramidal-shaped evergreen tree with low-lying spreaders fill a space differently than a loose, wide-oval or round shaped deciduous tree with no ground-hugging limbs. When selecting a tree for your front yard, it is important to choose one with a shape that suits your design.

Some trees sport fragrant spring blossoms, bear fruit, and turn color throughout the seasons. If the fruit is left on the branches to dry, its form and color contributes to the beauty of the specimen in the winter months.

The following chart gives an overall view of tree shapes. Study it and the following illustrations of trees to become familiar with the size, shape, and density of various varieties. Note also the leaf or needle texture of each tree.

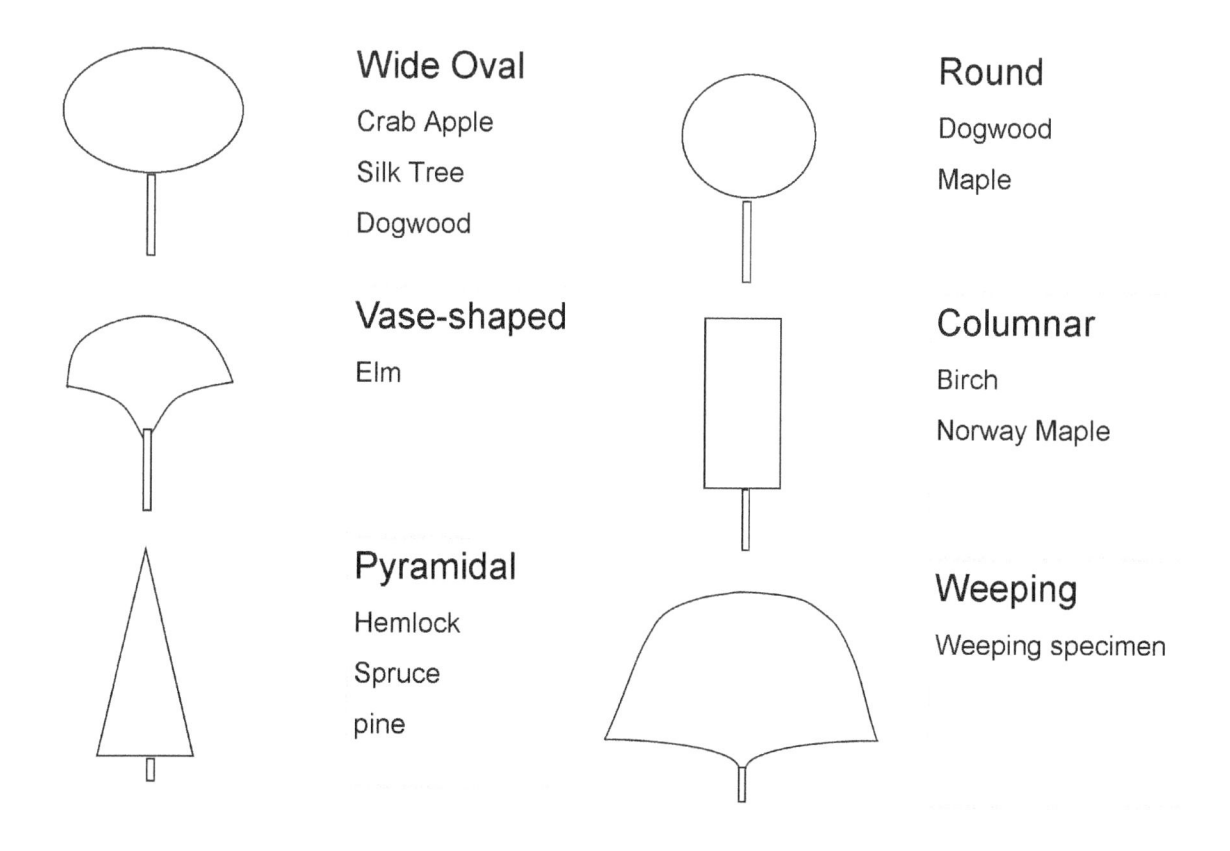

Wide Oval
Crab Apple
Silk Tree
Dogwood

Round
Dogwood
Maple

Vase-shaped
Elm

Columnar
Birch
Norway Maple

Pyramidal
Hemlock
Spruce
pine

Weeping
Weeping specimen

Deciduous

Coniferous

Adding Trees to a Front Yard

When adding trees to a front yard, consider the full-grown size of each tree. Also intersperse deciduous trees with coniferous which gives variety in shape, form and color and enjoy the beauty created as can be seen in these before and after pictures.

Here red maples are interspersed with blue spruce. Red maples will grow to form a round silhouette while the spruce forms a pyramidal silhouette with wide bottom spreaders.

Before: The sparseness of deciduous trees during the winter months begs for more varieties to be added.

The red maples will provide shade in the summer and the spruce will fill in gaps providing a wind break and year-round color. The red-colored leaves of the maples and the blue-green of the spruce play against each other to add interest as does the contrast between the large leaf of the maple and the needles of the spruce.

After: Interspersing the deciduous trees with coniferous trees adds interest and year round color.

Selecting a Specimen Tree

A specimen tree is a tree that is planted, not for the shade it gives, nor to break the wind, but as an accent plant. It is a smaller variety of tree with the added interest of colorful spring blossoms and colorful fruit, or sports an unusual shape, such as those that fit the category of weeping specimens.

A specimen tree is planted in a place where it will be noticed and enjoyed and often is the focal point of the garden.

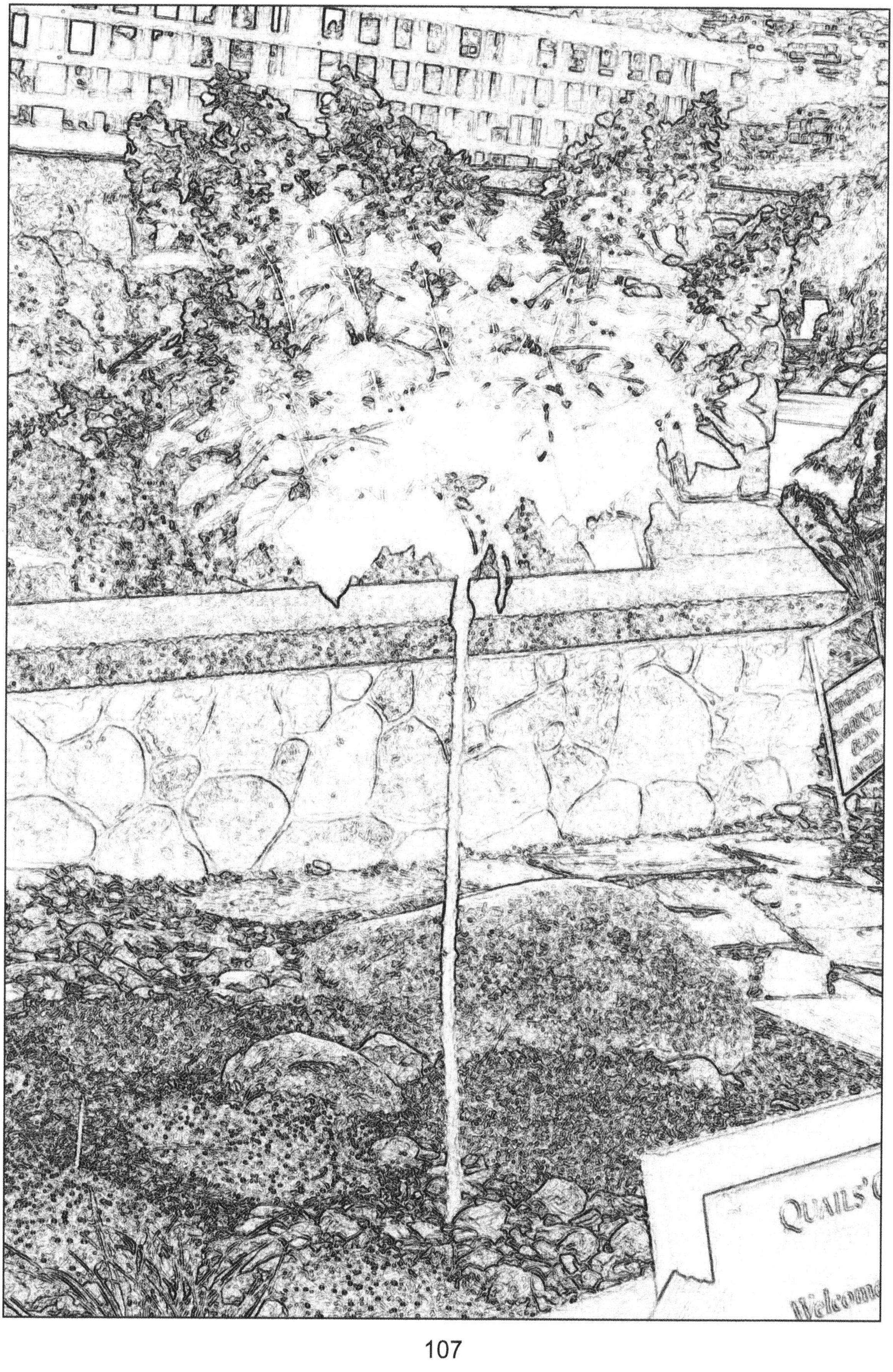
QUAILS'

Selecting Shrubs

Now we move on to selecting shrubs. While trees are a focal point to a garden, shrubs are supporting players. As with trees, shrubs fall into similar categories, deciduous and evergreen. Shrubs vary in size and shape. Some are large and loose while others are small, tight, and compact. Some branch upward, others branch outward, some sport weeping branches, and others creep along the ground. Deciduous shrubs are less dense than evergreens and some sport fragrant and colorful flowerettes.

Deciduous shrubs vary in color from dark to light green, blue, red, purple, yellow, and a variety of mixes of these colors, and although coniferous evergreens stay within the greens, their hues range from deep, dark, greens to lighter greens, to blue-greens which add impact to the planting bed.

Study the following Shrub Shapes chart and observe the following when considering shrubs in a planting bed.

1. The size and shape
2. Branching structure
3. Foliage, flower, fruit, and branch or needle color
4. Hardiness

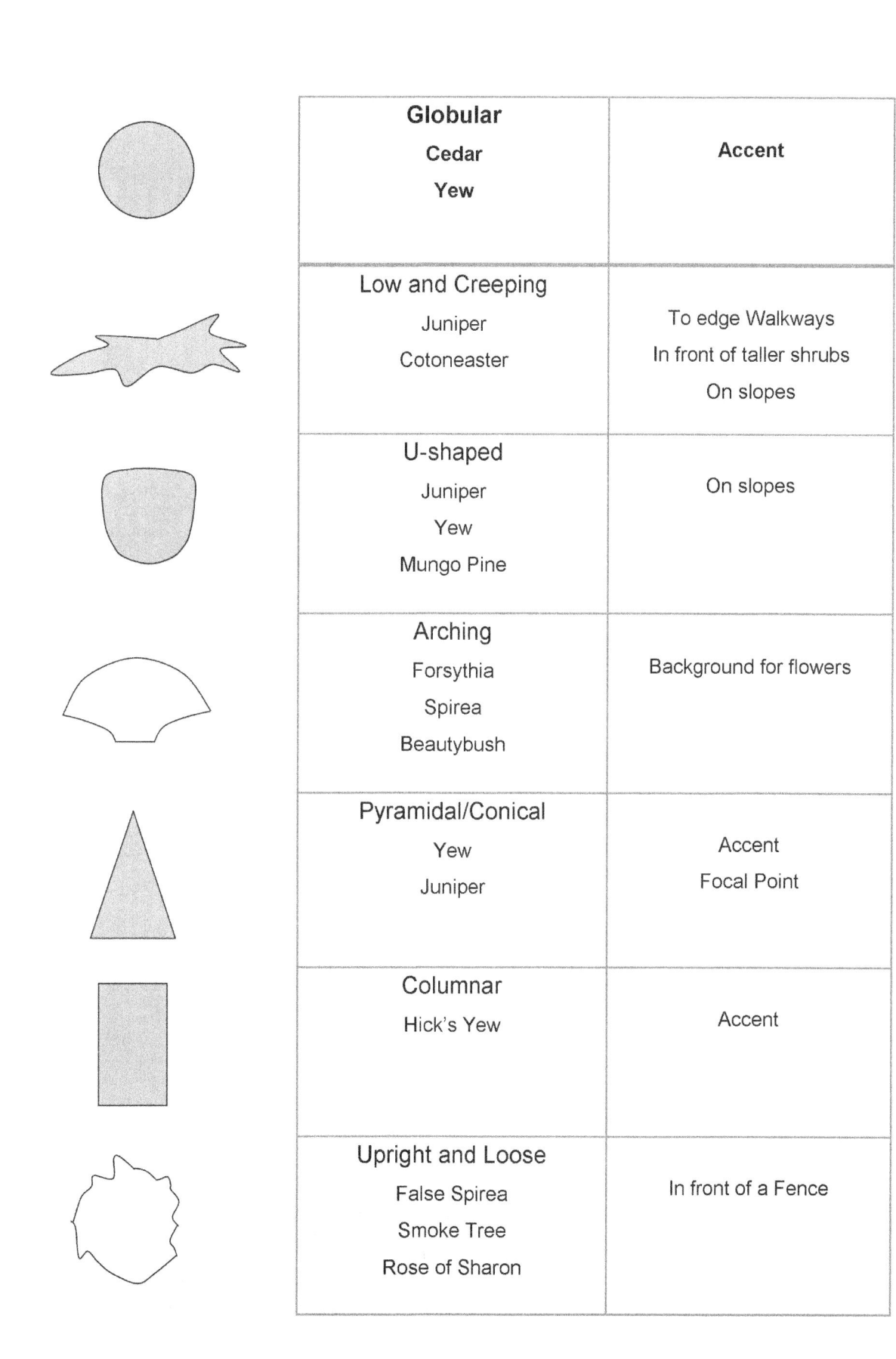

●	**Globular** Cedar Yew	Accent
✦	**Low and Creeping** Juniper Cotoneaster	To edge Walkways In front of taller shrubs On slopes
⬭	**U-shaped** Juniper Yew Mungo Pine	On slopes
⌒	**Arching** Forsythia Spirea Beautybush	Background for flowers
▲	**Pyramidal/Conical** Yew Juniper	Accent Focal Point
▮	**Columnar** Hick's Yew	Accent
✿	**Upright and Loose** False Spirea Smoke Tree Rose of Sharon	In front of a Fence

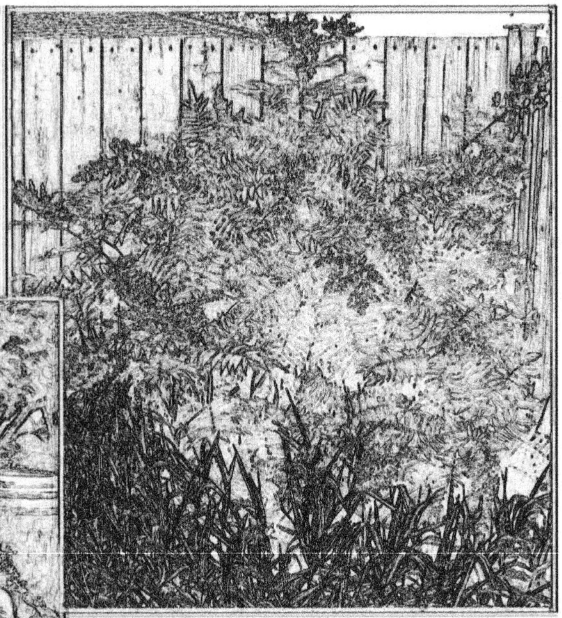

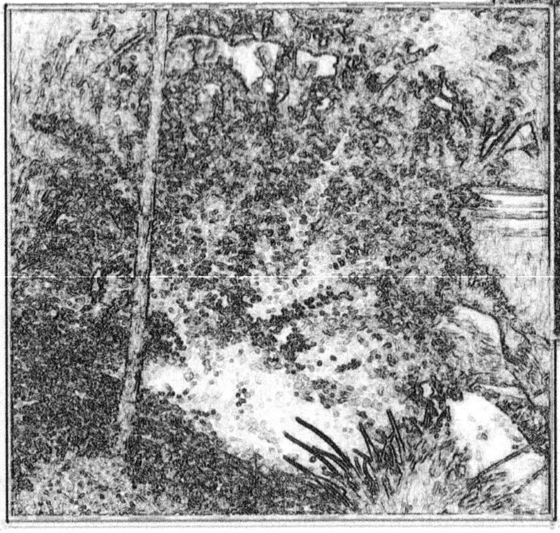

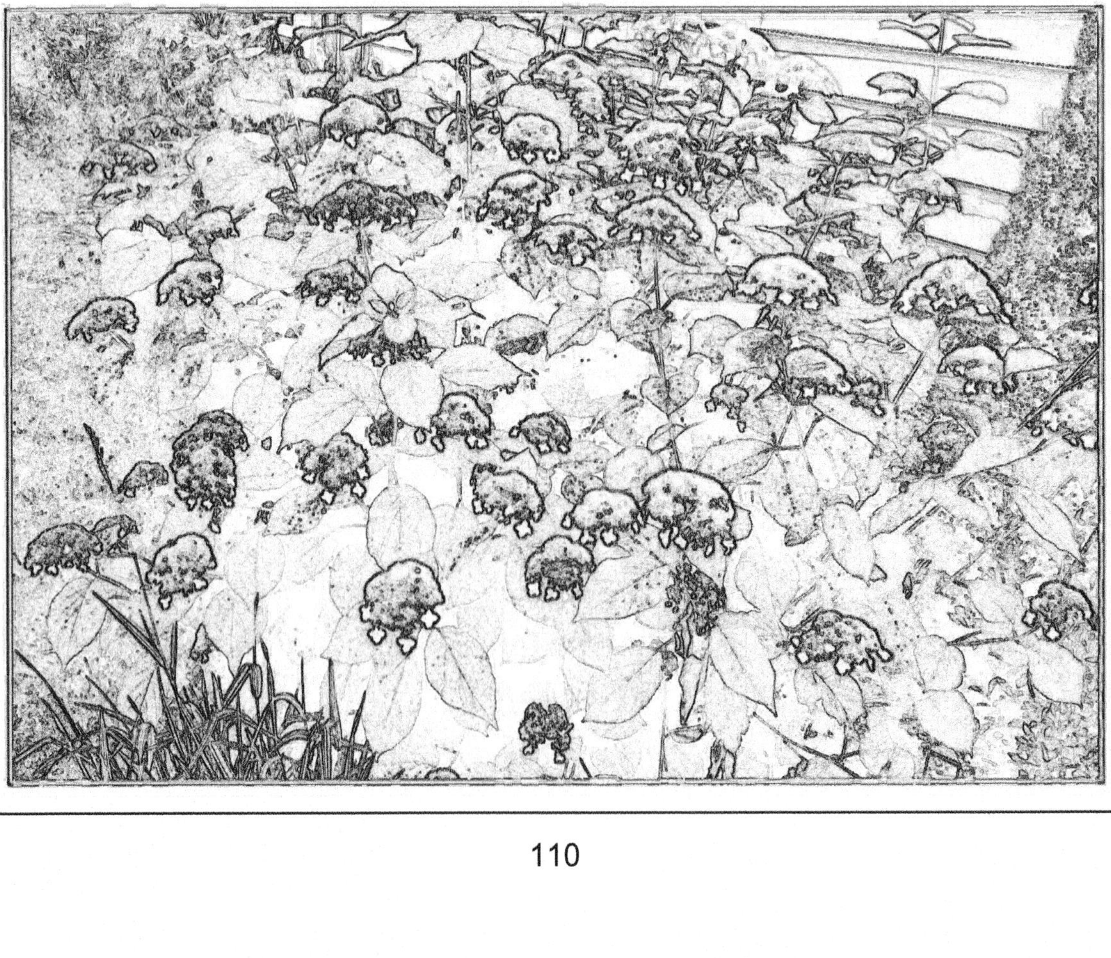

111

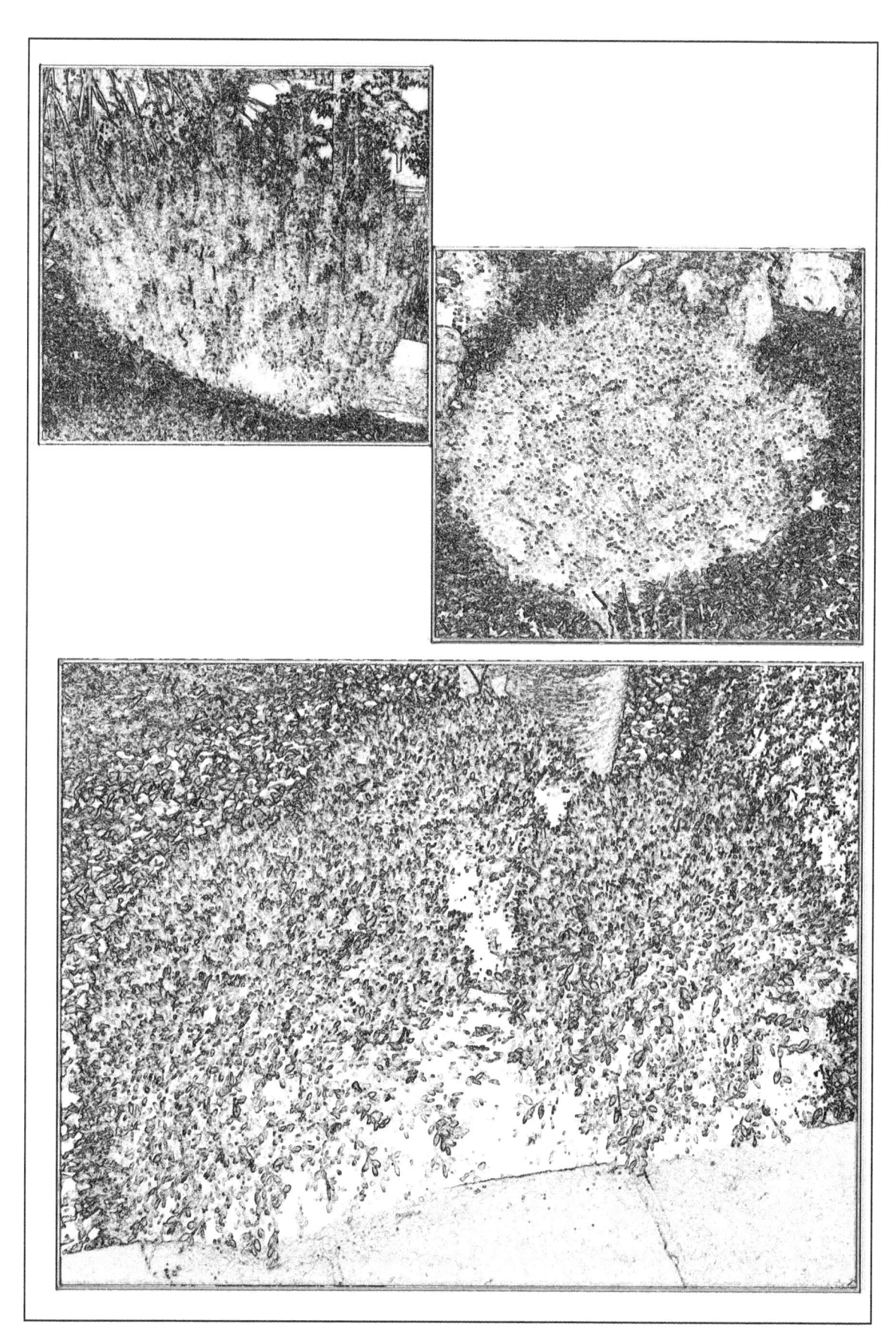

Adding Vines

Vines can be added into the front yard garden design. Placement of a vine beside a front entrance accents the front door. A clinging vine will grow up against a bare brick or stone wall, however, other species of vines need to be planted against a trellis. A decorative trellis, such as the one shown in this illustration, can contribute another element of beauty to the garden.

Designing With Perennials

Not only are trees and shrubs good choices for a front yard garden, but also are perennials. A perennial is a flowering plant that dies back in the winter and blooms again the following summer. These hardy flowing plants add depth and interest to the planting bed. When choosing perennials for your garden, observe their following attributes.

- The flowers of spring blooming perennials add color to your garden throughout the spring season, those of summer blooming perennials add color throughout the summer season, and those of fall blooming perennials add color during the fall season. Some perennials continue to bloom throughout the spring, summer, and fall.

- Perennials contribute an unending variety of foliage color, shape, and texture to your garden.

Perennial Beds and Borders

Perennials work well in a planting bed and in a border along a walkway or up against a fence. To gain the most of your perennials, keep the following in mind. Dark colors are strong and should be used sparingly, while pale, pastel colors can be used more frequently. This includes both leaf and flower color.

To keep the bed or border in bloom throughout the spring, summer, and fall for a continuous display of color, choose perennials with different blooming times.

When working with flower color, choose perennials flowers in a palette that blends well. Do not fill the garden with an array of randomly colored blooms. Be selective. Choose two to three colors that work well together and repeat them throughout the bed. Color combos that go well together are pinks and violets with white or yellows. For a warmer palette, choose muted oranges mixed with yellows. Use bright colors such as oranges or reds, sparingly and just to add a punch of color so as not to be overwhelming. White blooms can be added into any palette, as white is neutral.

When choosing perennials for your garden, don't forget to consider leaf color, shape and texture. These elements contribute to creating an outstanding display.

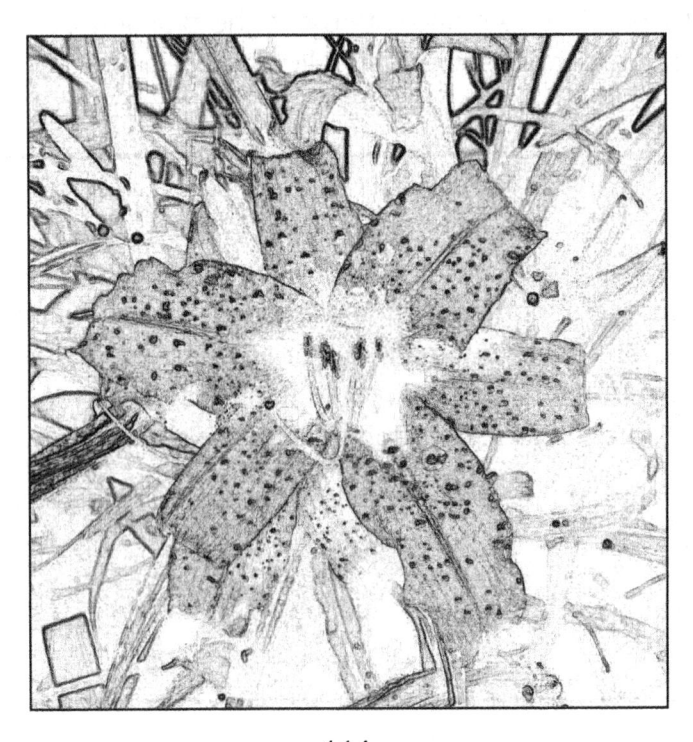

In the following planting example, tall, rigid-stemmed irises with thick, dark-toned blade-like leaves attract the eye, and are positioned in the center of the planting bed to become a focal point. Contrasting blue-green, broad-leafed hostas of intermediate height and with an alternate flower shape are massed around them. At the edges of the planting bed, and filling in around the base of intermediate plantings are brightly colored tiny-flowered coreopsis, shorter specimens with differing flower and foliage color.

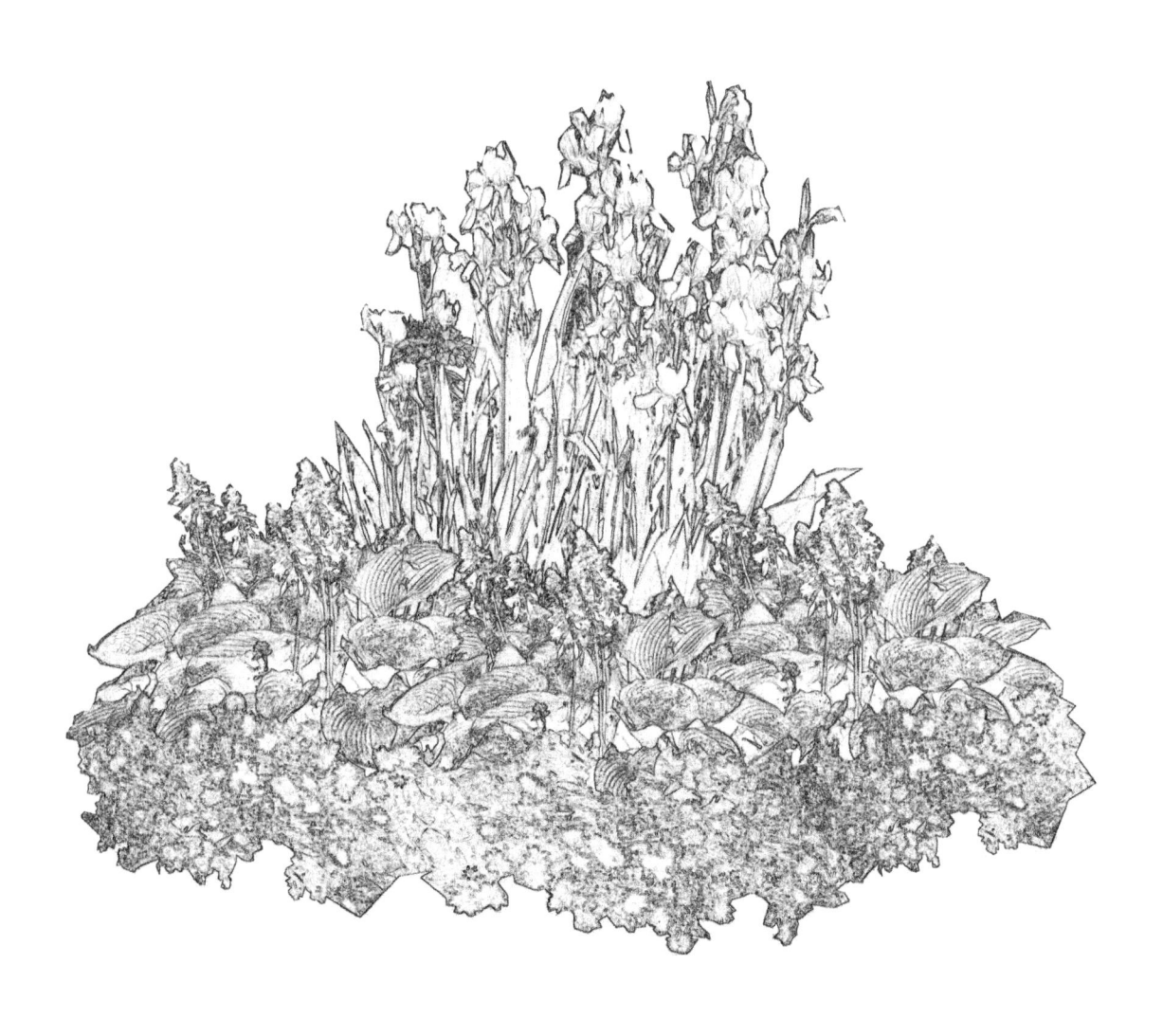

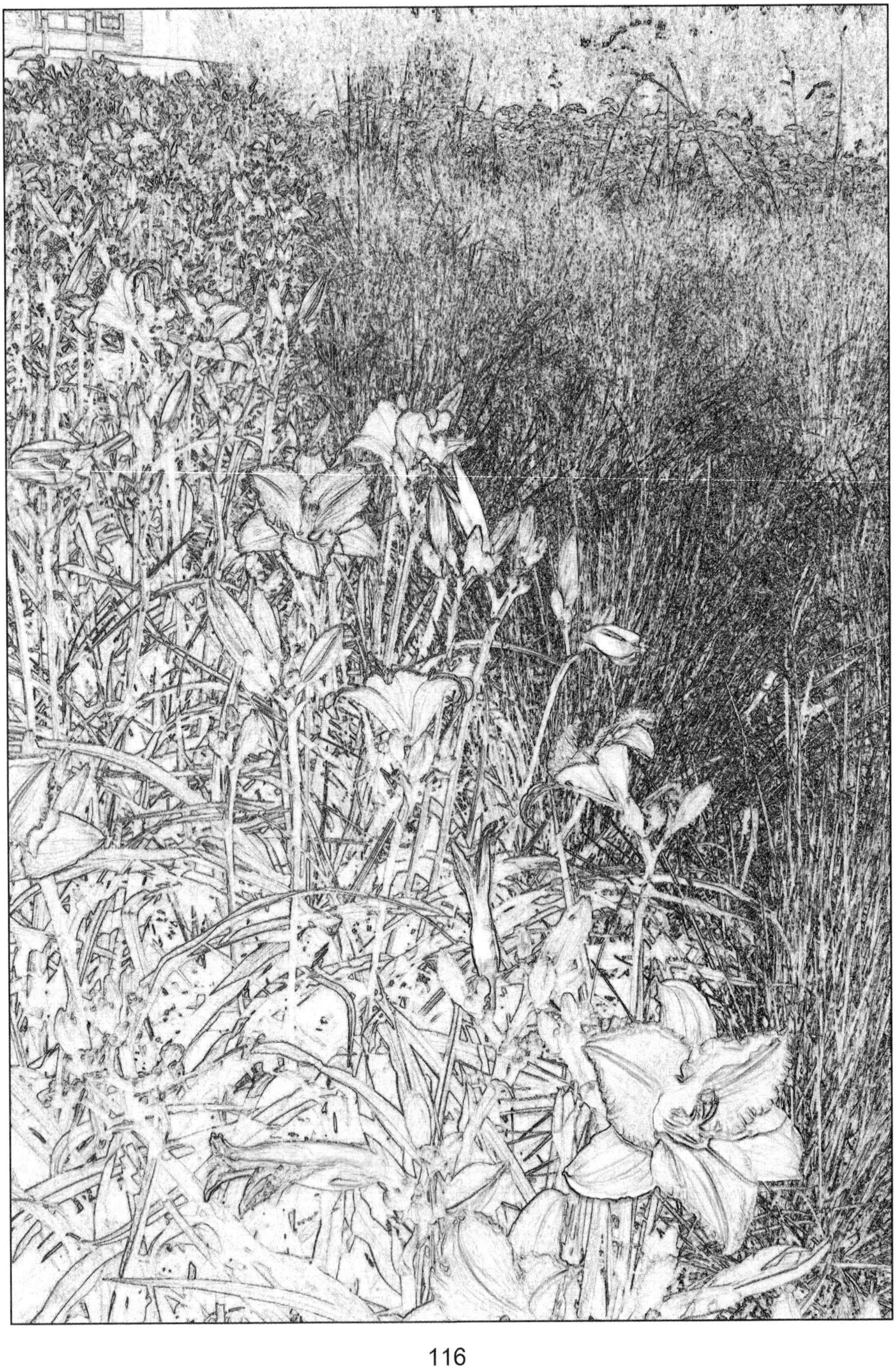

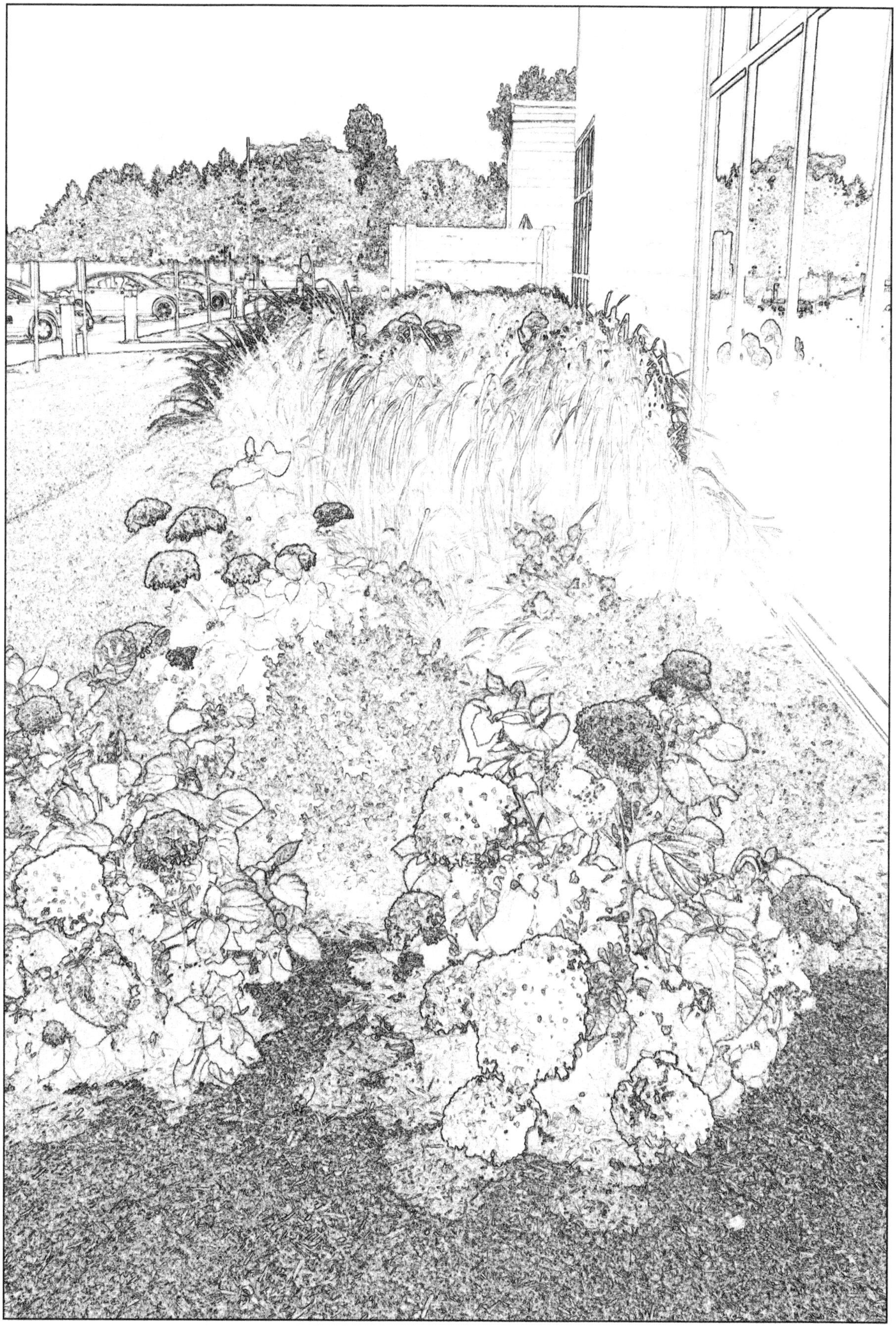

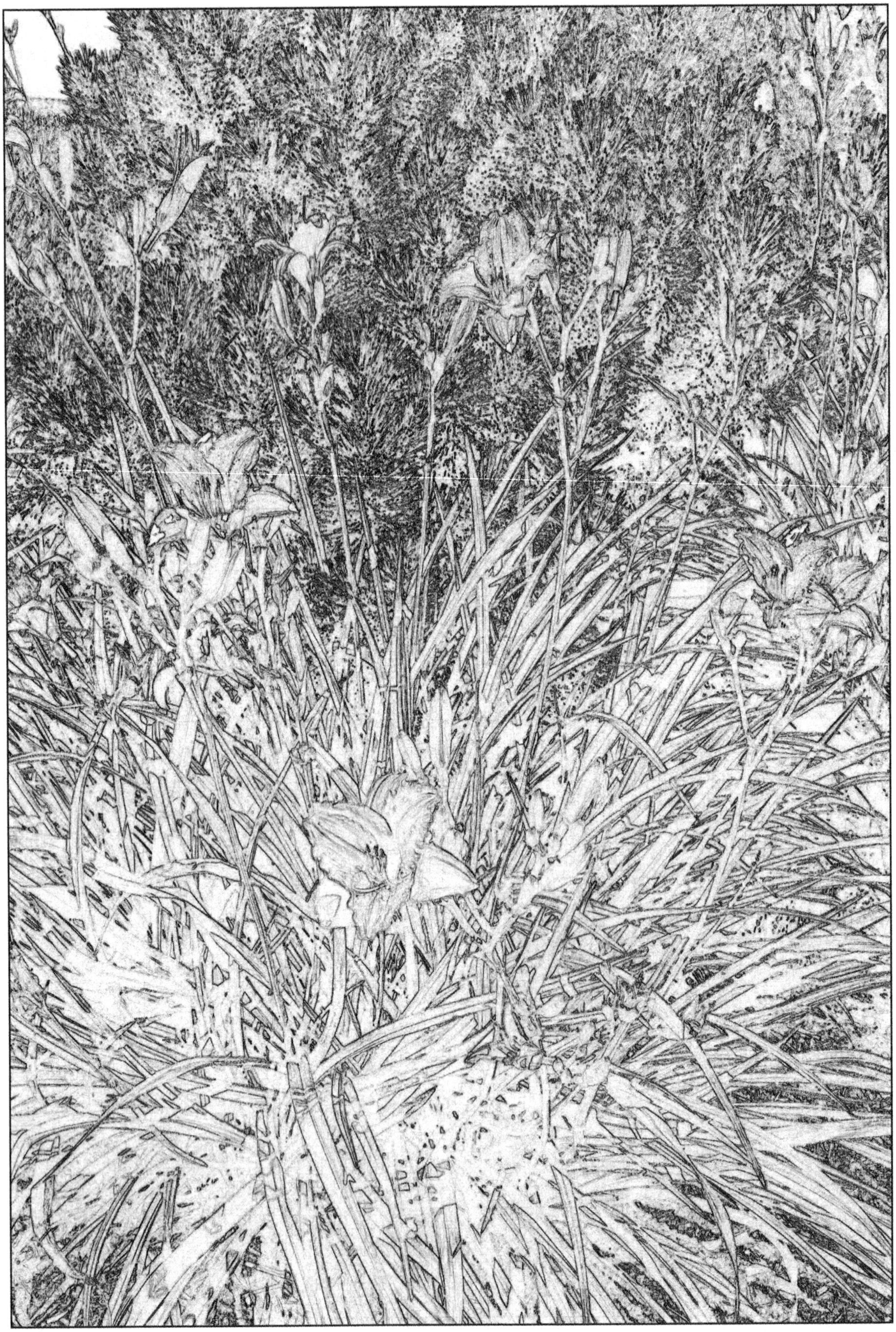

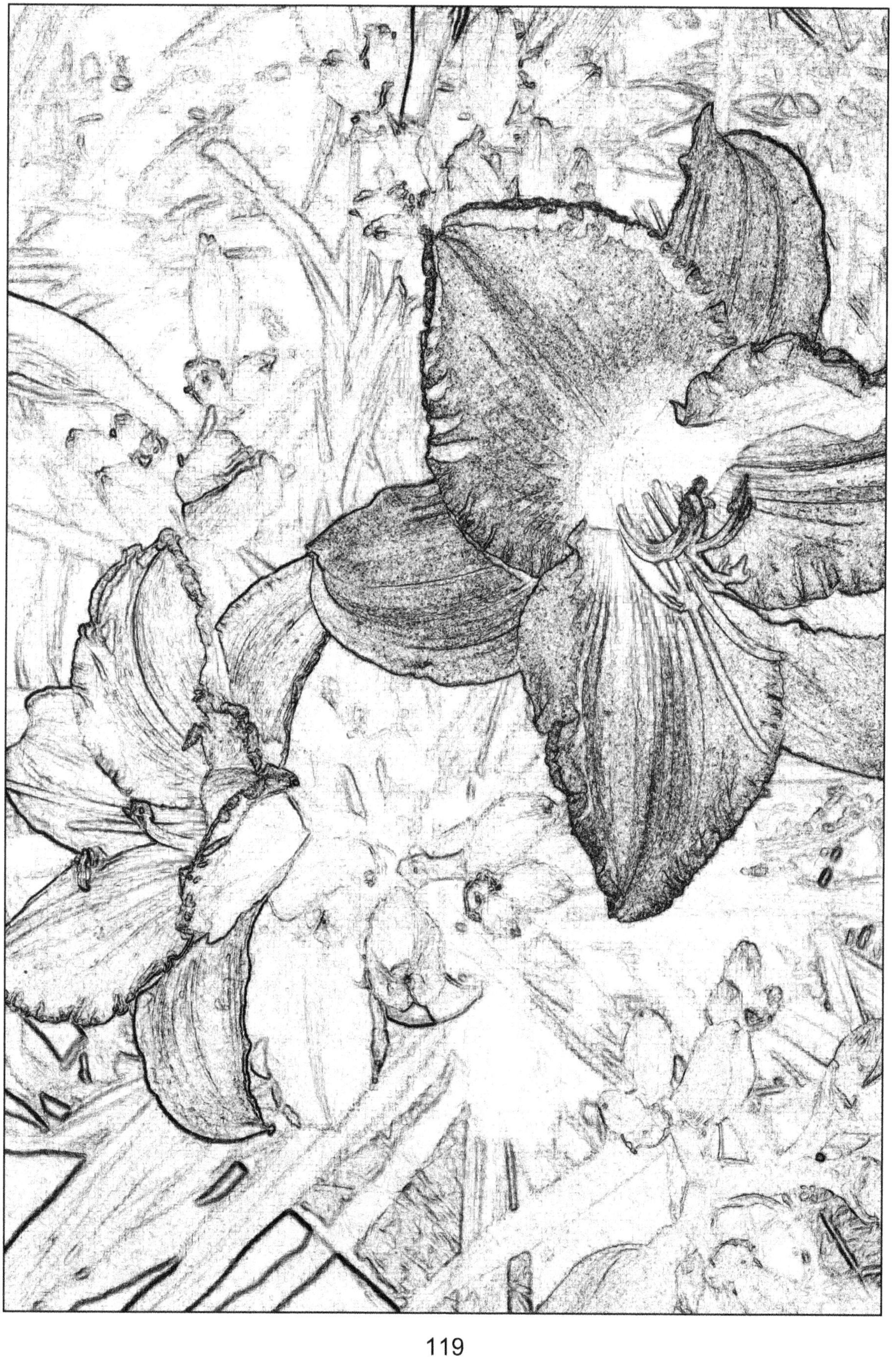

Common Perennials A

Bergenia Sun or shade with moist, loamy soil

Broad-leafed Hosta
Prefers shade and moist, loamy soil

Lady's Mantle
Prefers sun and dry to moist loam

Fern Prefers shade and moist, loamy soil

Common Perennials B

Gooseneck Loosestrife
Sun or shade, moist, loamy soil

Liatris "Blazing Star"
Sun with moist, loamy soil

Day Lily
Sun with moist, loamy soil

Common Perennials C

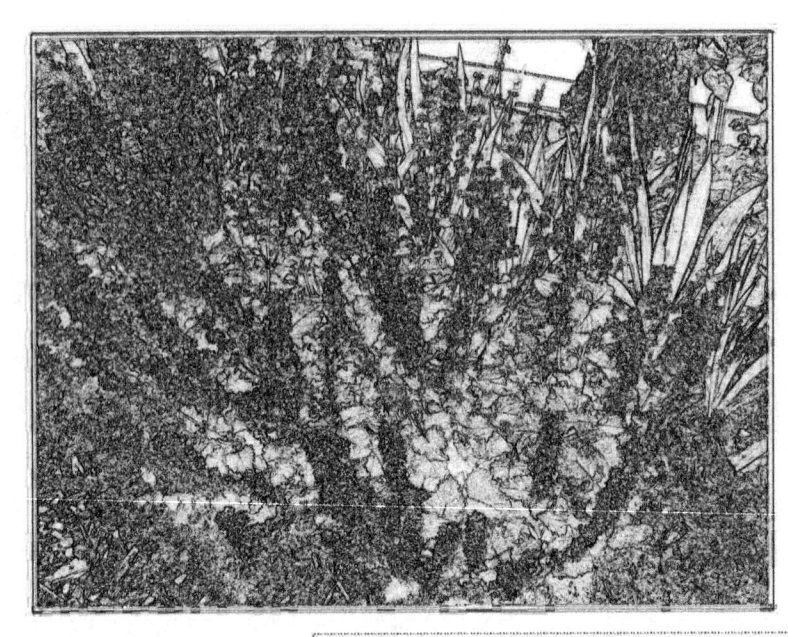

Salvia Prefers full sun and sandy loam

Variegated Day Lily
Prefers full sun and loamy soil

Rose Prefers sun and loamy soil

Common Perennials D

Coral Bells
Full sun and moist loam

Ligularia
Prefers shade and moist loamy soil

Astilbe Prefers shade and moist, loamy soil

Common Perennials E

Cat Mint
Prefers full sun and dry loam

Lamb's Ear
Prefers full sun and sandy loam

Spiderwort
Prefers full sun to partial shade and moist loam

Common Perennials F

Violet Sage
Prefers full sun and dry loam

Sedum
Prefers full sun and dry loam

Russian Sage
Prefers full sun and dry sandy loam

Designing With Perennial Grasses

Designing with perennial grasses gives a much different feel to a garden than does designing with flowering perennials. Grasses come in a variety of different shapes and sizes just as flowering perennials do, and the highlight of grasses is their form and texture, as well as their color. When mixed with flowering perennials, they put on a wispy and wonderful display.

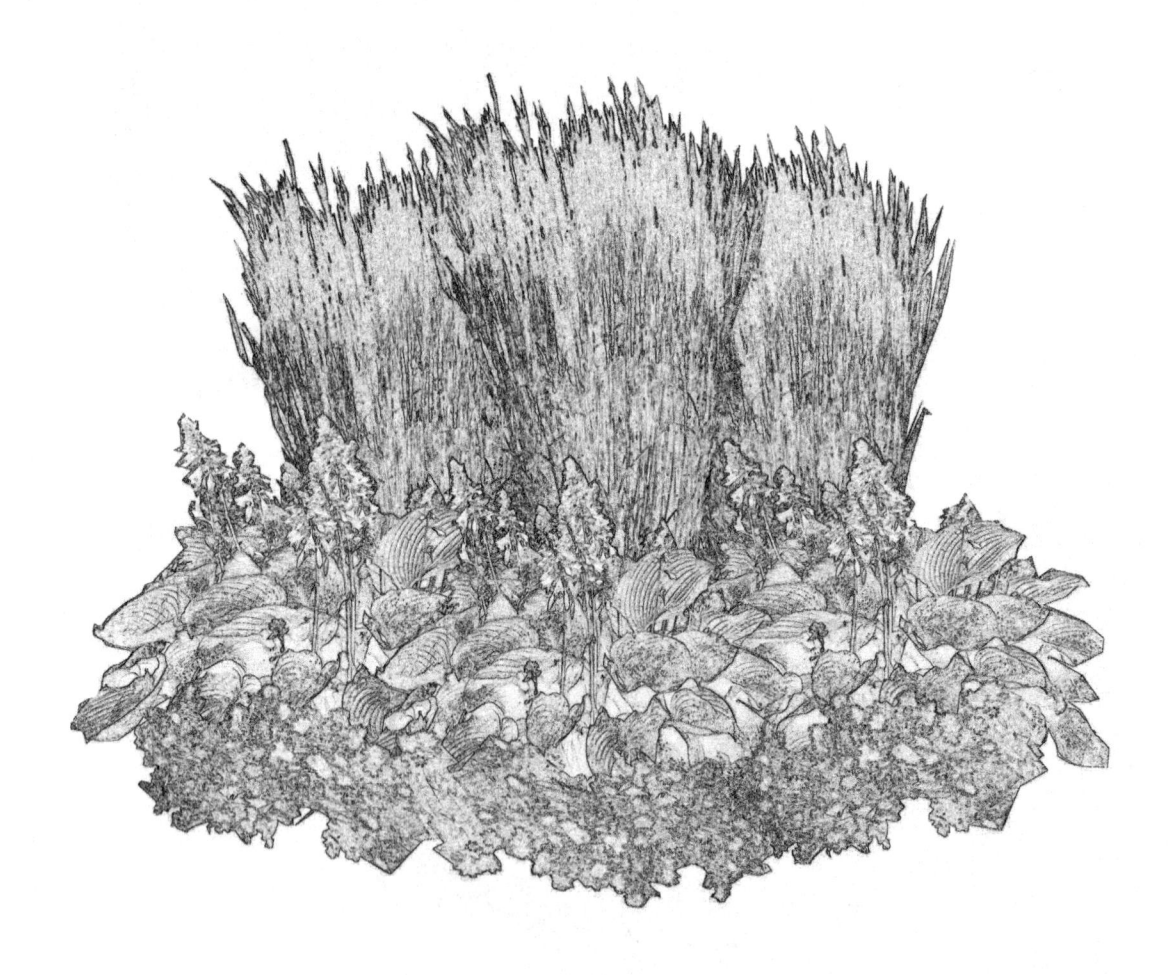

Designing With Perennial Grasses A

Designing With Perennial Grasses B

Designing With Annuals

Annuals are flowering plants that bloom throughout the summer season but cannot tolerate freezing temperatures, therefore their impact can be enjoyed all season long, but they will have to be replaced each year.

Annuals are best displayed in patio and garden planters where their environment of sun and soil conditions can be controlled, however some varieties do well planted directly into a prepared planting bed that has been enriched with compost or loamy topsoil.

Annuals provide a mat of color when planted along the edges of a walkway or when massed around the base of other plantings. Deadheading blooms as they die out prompts the plant to flower more profusely.

Annuals can be purchased from your local nursery and planted as soon as the ground is warm enough in the spring and there is no more night frost. When choosing your annuals, keep in mind the principle of color-coordination and plant those that fit your color palette.

Adding Container Gardens

Container gardens add bursts of color to an otherwise boring space. They help to fill in what is missing in your already perfected landscape scheme. Set them onto your deck, patio, tucked into a garden bed, or along garden paths to add impact, draw attention, and warrant a second look. No outdoor space is complete without them.

Patio pots filled with colorful annual, and sometimes perennial, blooms can be purchased at your local garden venue. You don't have to plant them yourself, but if you are so inclined, there are a few things you need to consider.

First of all you will need to decide on their location in your landscape. Will they sit in full sun out on a patio, or be tucked into a shady corner? Some plants prefer full sun with 8-12 hours per day, others part sun with 4-8 hours, and still others prefer mostly shade with 2-4 hours of morning or late afternoon sun. Therefore, it is vital to choose plantings that will suit their need for the sun or shade. Even those that love sun, cannot be in direct noon sun without scorching, so finding a spot on your patio or in your garden where there is some shade is helpful to keeping plantings flourishing. Examples of good full-sun varieties to add to your planters include Super Spike, Salvia, Nicotiana, Fountain Grass, Lobelia, Coleus, Ivy Geranium, Vinca and Sweet Potato Vine, Ivy, Scaveola, Petunia, Verbena, Portulaca, Creeping Zinnia, Lantana, and Lobelia. Part-sun picks include all the above with the exception of Lobelia and Lantana, but with the addition of Geranium and Impatiens.

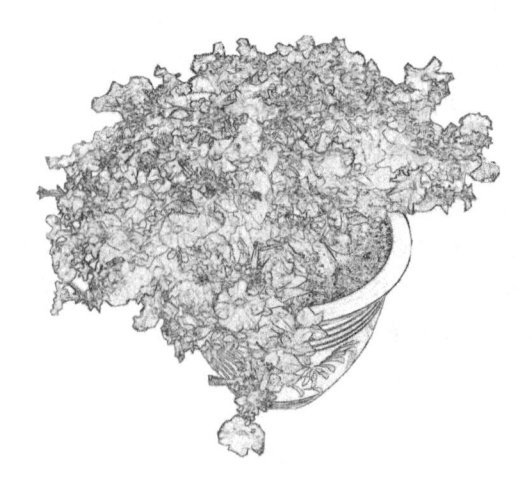

Shade lovers include Super Spike, Impatiens, Begonia, Asparagus Fern, Plectranthus, Ivy, Vinca Vine, Coleus, Impatiens, Fuchsia, and Caladium.

When choosing your plants, keep in mind design attributes. Use your ingenuity to create a beautifully colorful display with consideration of plant height and texture, as well as growth habit. Almost every container garden benefits by the addition of swirling, trailing specimens, but these can be omitted and still have good results. Because a patio pot is seen on all sides, it needs to be evenly filled and balanced from all directions. Usually a large-growing specimen is planted in the center of the pot, but not always, and smaller-growing specimens surround it. The overall look is to be balanced, and that can be achieved by filling the planter with several plants of the same species, but that does not mean you are limited to using the same base plants all around. As a matter of fact, greater interest is created by mixing varieties.

For example, for a sunny to part-sunny location, start by planting your tallest species in the center of your container, such as Super Spike, Fountain Grass, or Salvia. Work outward to include a mix of Petunia, Verbena, and Lobelia. Finish around the outside edges of the pot with a trailing ivy or Sweet Potato Vine. For a shade pot, begin with Super Spike or Fern and plant around with Begonia and Impatiens, and finish edging with ivy.

Now that you know what plants to use, it is time to choose your container, prepare your soil, plant, water, and fertilize your garden. Containers come in a variety of colors, styles, shapes and sizes. Some are made of plastic, while others of rot-resistant wood, ceramic, concrete, or clay. Choose a pot that fits your liking, making sure it is large enough to efficiently support the root systems of your plantings as they grow.

It is important to use the best soil you can afford. It will guarantee beautiful blooms and healthy plants. Use prepackaged potting soil or a combination of garden soil, peat moss, and sand or vermiculite to provide good drainage. Add 10-52-10 plant starter and water in after potting.

So finally you can enjoy the beauty of your newly planted container garden. From this point on, all you have to do is care for its needs to keep it healthy. Because of the small size provided by a planter compared with planting directly into a garden bed, limits are set on your plants' opportunity for food and water, therefore regular waterings and feedings, as well as some practical maintenance is required. Although shade varieties can do with less, sun and partial-sun varieties need daily waterings to keep them from completely drying out, and fertilizer needs to be applied weekly to provide nutrients. Along with food and water, flowering plants need to be deadheaded on a regular basis to encourage continuous blooming and weeds need to be pulled to prevent unnecessary absorption of water and nutrients by these culprits.

Apart from container gardens offering abundant color and beauty to your landscape, they have the added benefit of being portable. They can be moved around and into place if for some reason they are not thriving in the location you have chosen for them. If they are wilting and browning in too much sun, move them into a shadier spot. If they aren't blooming and flourishing as they should, try transporting them into a sunnier location. Once you find the exact conditions, along with proper care, you can enjoy the beauty of your container gardens all season long!

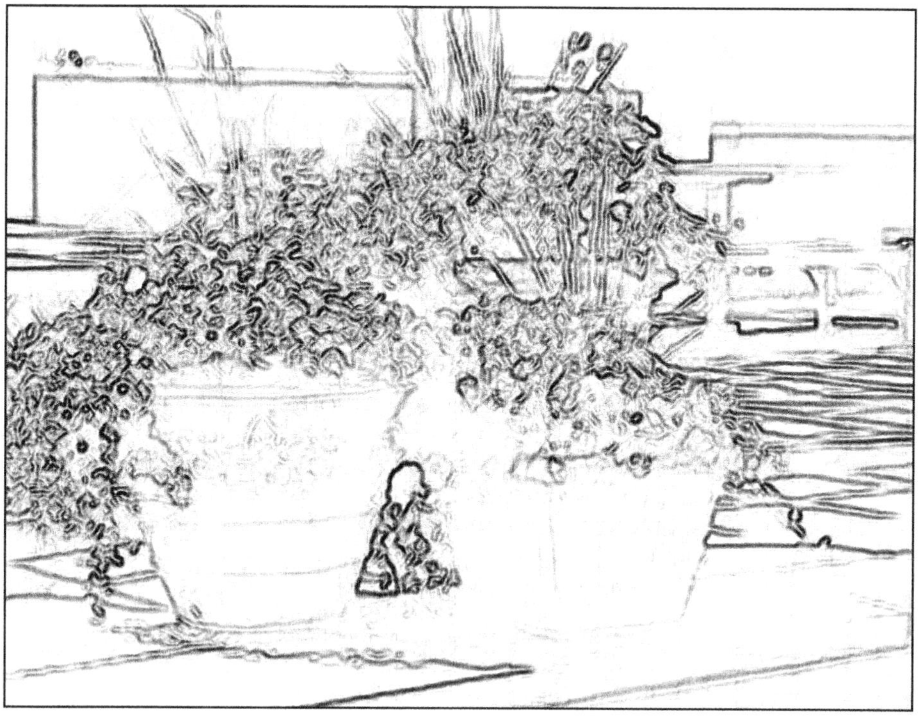

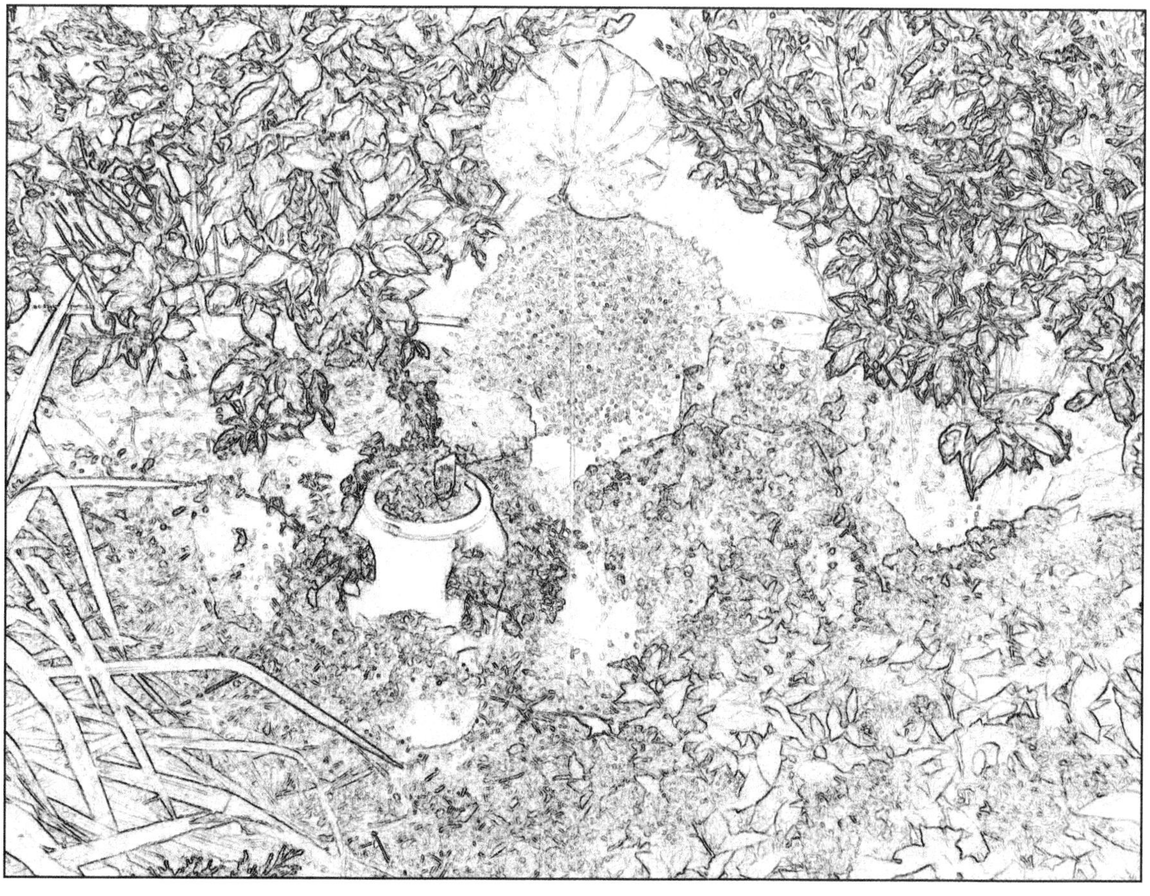

Adding Hanging Baskets

Hanging flowers in baskets is another way to enhance your landscape. Instead of taking up space in the garden, they can be displayed from a variety of locations in your yard to add still another dimension of beauty.

Just as with container gardens, hanging baskets are filled with colorful annuals that keep blooming throughout the summer season. And just as container gardens, if hung fairly low, look best with a tall upright center plant, smaller varieties massing outwards, and those that hang down and trail over the edges. If however, the basket is to be hung higher than eye-level, the tall center plant should be omitted with emphasis put on achieving a more rounded contour.

. Choosing a container for your hanging display is a little more complex than it is for patio display. You have various similar mediums of plastic and wood to choose from with a straightforward method of filling with soil and planting, but also others that require special attention when planting. One of these is a wire basket. The advantage of a wire basket is that plants can be planted into its sides at different intervals to form a fuller, more all-encompassing mass of flowers that surround the whole container as well as trail downwards.

To plant into a wire basket, a liner is needed to keep the soil from washing out. A good choice for lining is sphagnum moss, cocoa fiber, or other straw-like material. Pre-formed liners are available at your local garden center and can be cut to fit. Once the liner is in, holes can be made through the fibers from the sides of the basket and plants inserted from outside to in, root first. To prevent damage to the roots, wrap with tissue prior to inserting and remove tissue once in place. After the sides are planted, add soil to within an inch of the top of the container, and continue to plant from the top. When all plants are in place, water generously to settle the soil around the roots.

To get your baskets off to a good start, use lightweight packaged potting soil with equal parts vermiculite, perlite, and peat moss, and which contains a slow-release fertilizer. Choose and arrange plants to maximize their beauty, either filling your basket with a single variety or combining two or three varieties that flower at different times for more interest, making sure not to overplant, but providing room enough for their growth and spread. Good mounding plant choices for hanging baskets are alyssum, wax begonia, impatiens, pansies and brachyscome. Those that trail include verbena, ivy, scavola, sweet potato vine, trailing petunia, lysimachia and calibrachoa.

Hanging baskets look great suspended outward from a fence, pole, or corner of a building, making sure that wherever you locate them they will not pose a hazard. If suspended overhead, keep them high enough to be walked under, or if positioned outward, make sure they do not block walkways or interfere with other functions around the yard. Hang a series together at eye level for most visual impact or suspend them over an existing garden. Use them to enhance your front entrance by hanging them on display just outside your front door or at intervals along the length of a front porch. Here they will provide you with an abundant display of color as well as create a sense of privacy. Wherever you place them in your landscape, you can be sure they will add greatly to the curb appeal of your home.

Keep your hanging baskets looking their best all season long with a few maintenance tips. Water, water, water. Keep them from drying out with consistent and frequent watering, fertilize weekly, cut tips back regularly to encourage fuller and consistent flowering, and faithfully deadhead as flowers fade. Follow these tips and you will enjoy a beautiful display all summer long!

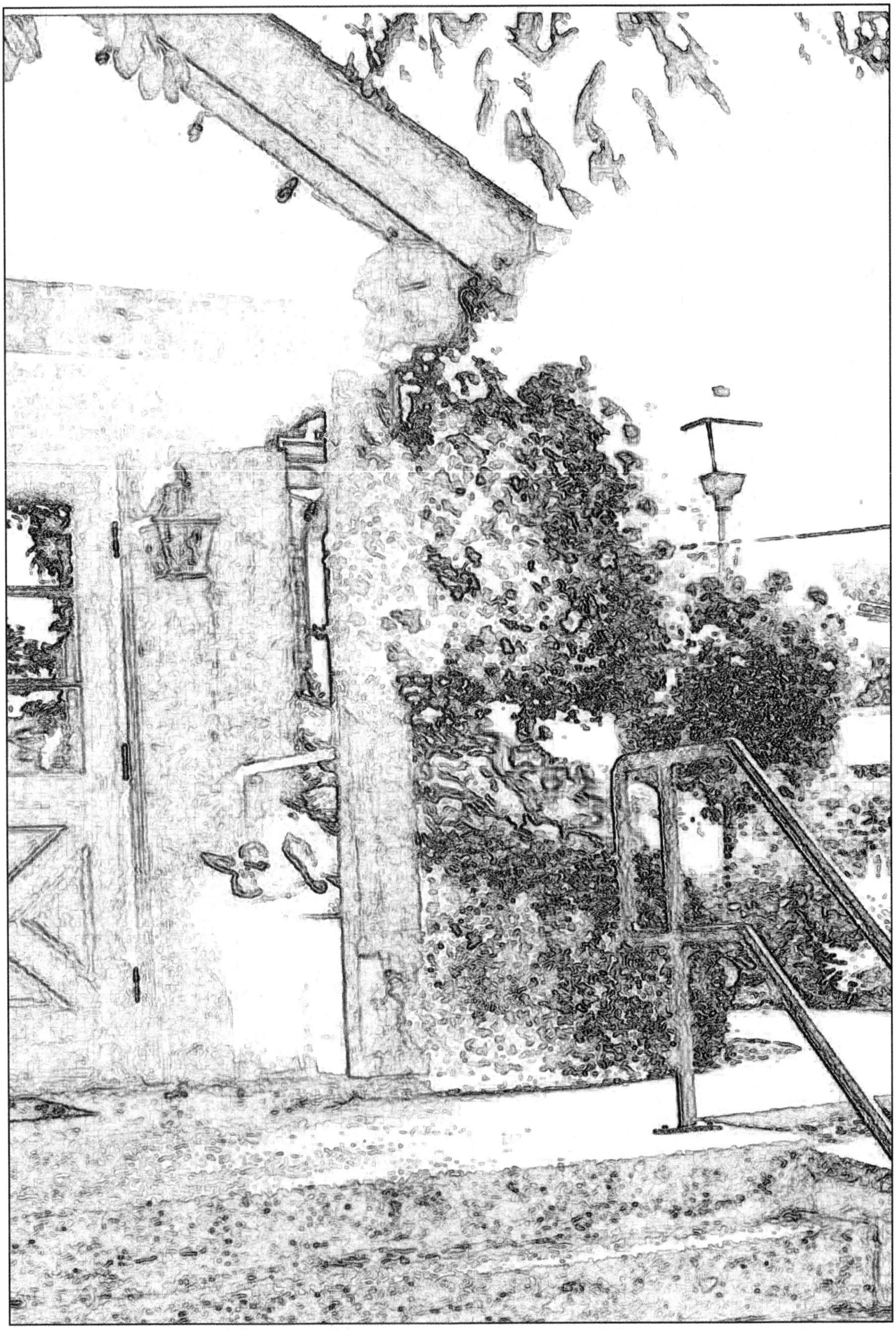

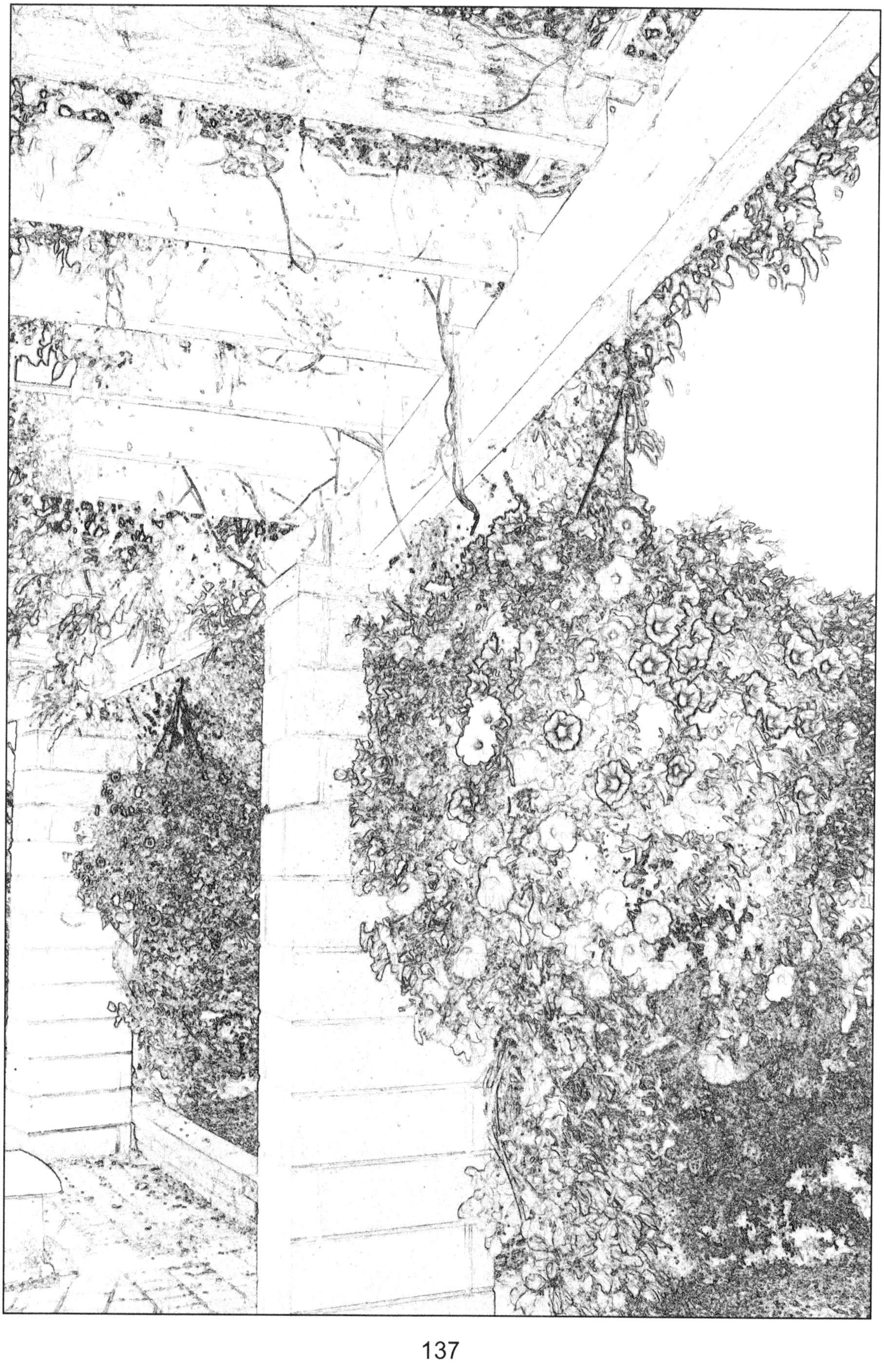

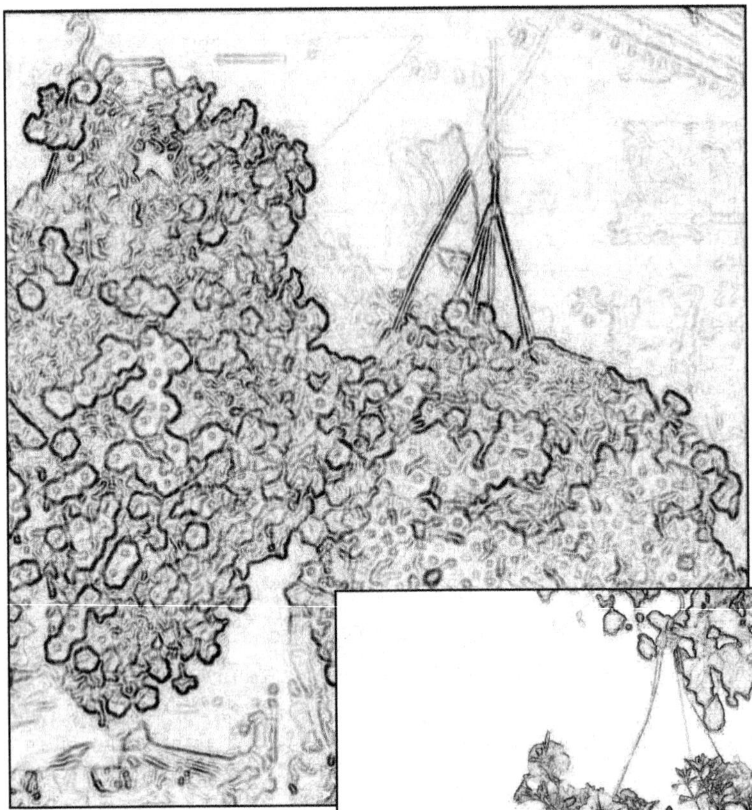

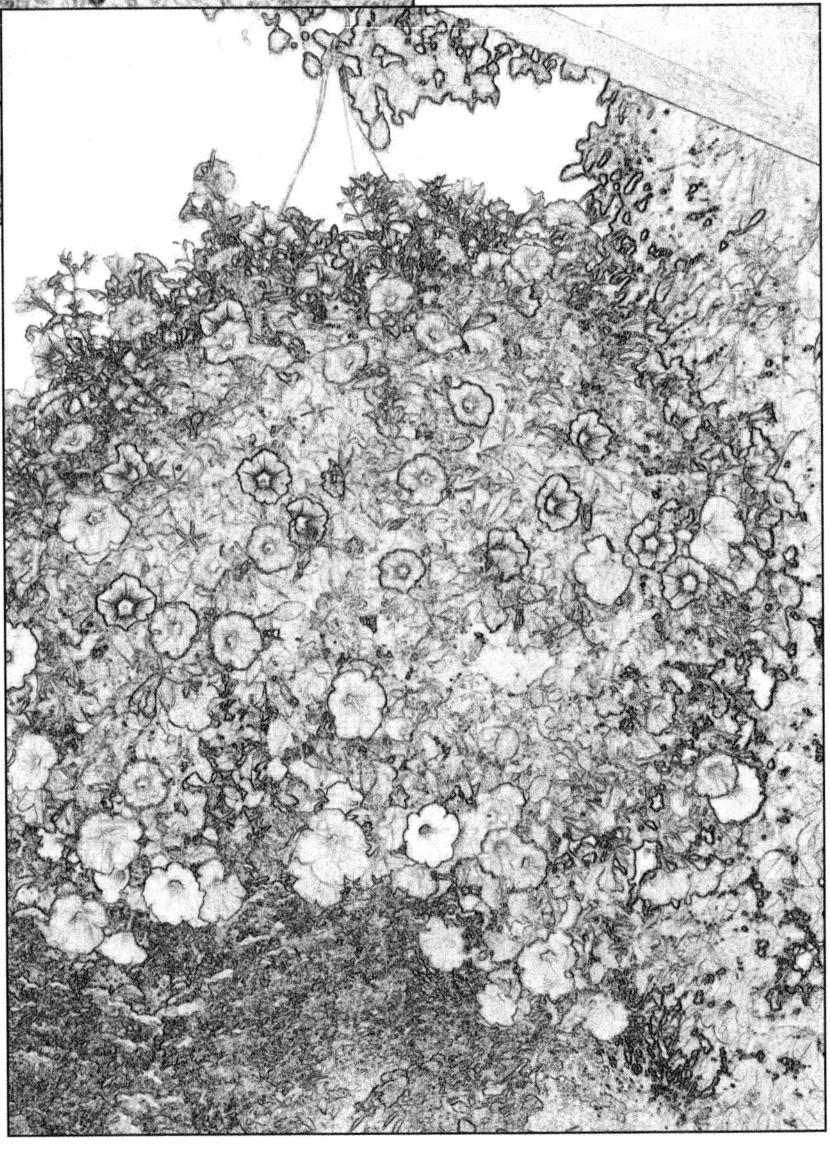

Garden Accents

Enhance your garden by adding accents of non-plant material such as garden art and lighting or add planted pots to patios, decks, and walkways. Add hanging baskets to fences to interject even more interest to your garden. If your design is an informal, cottage-style garden, consider adding elements from nature, such as wood stumps, to your garden decor. Study the next few photos to see how you can use these accents to enhance your front yard gardens.

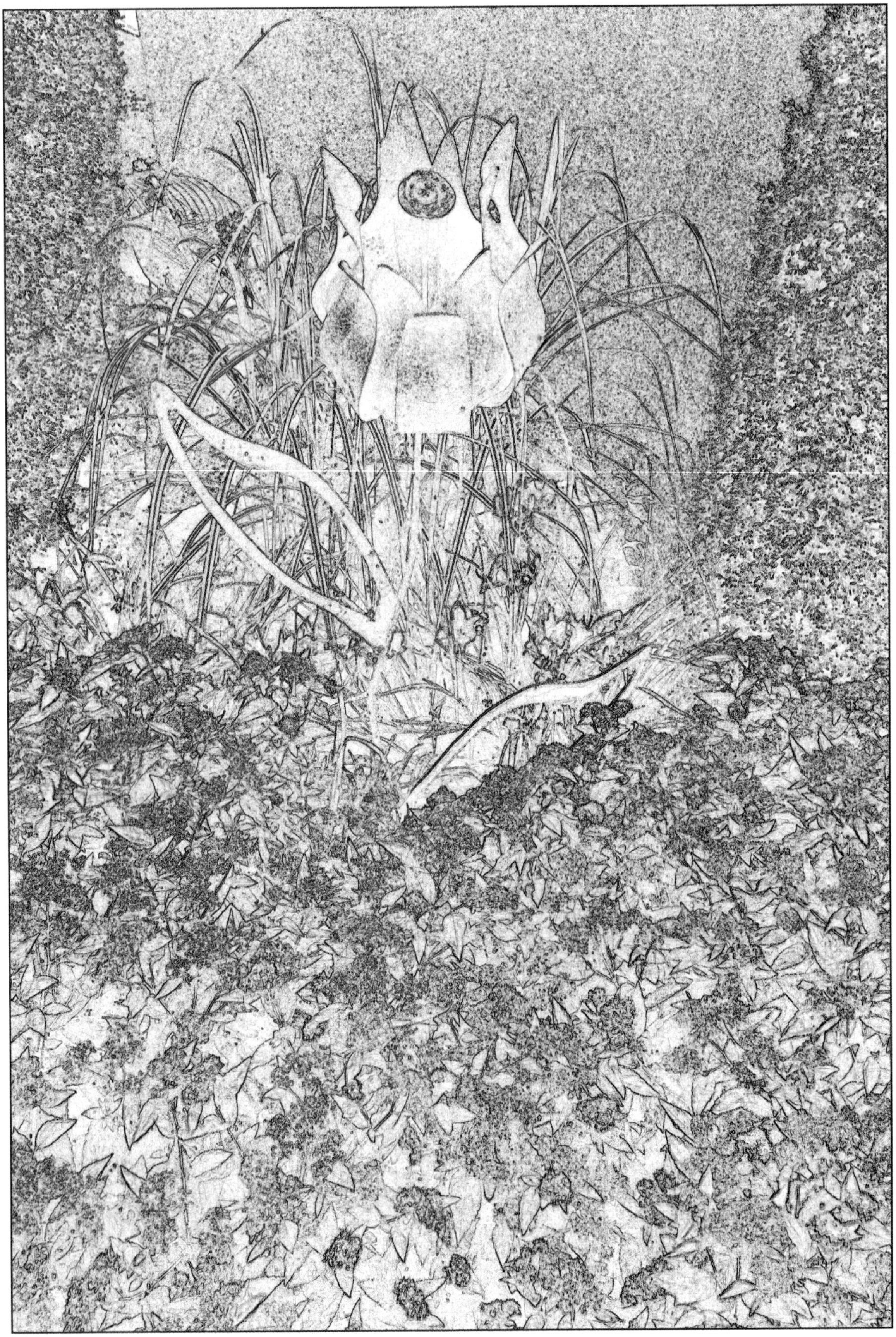

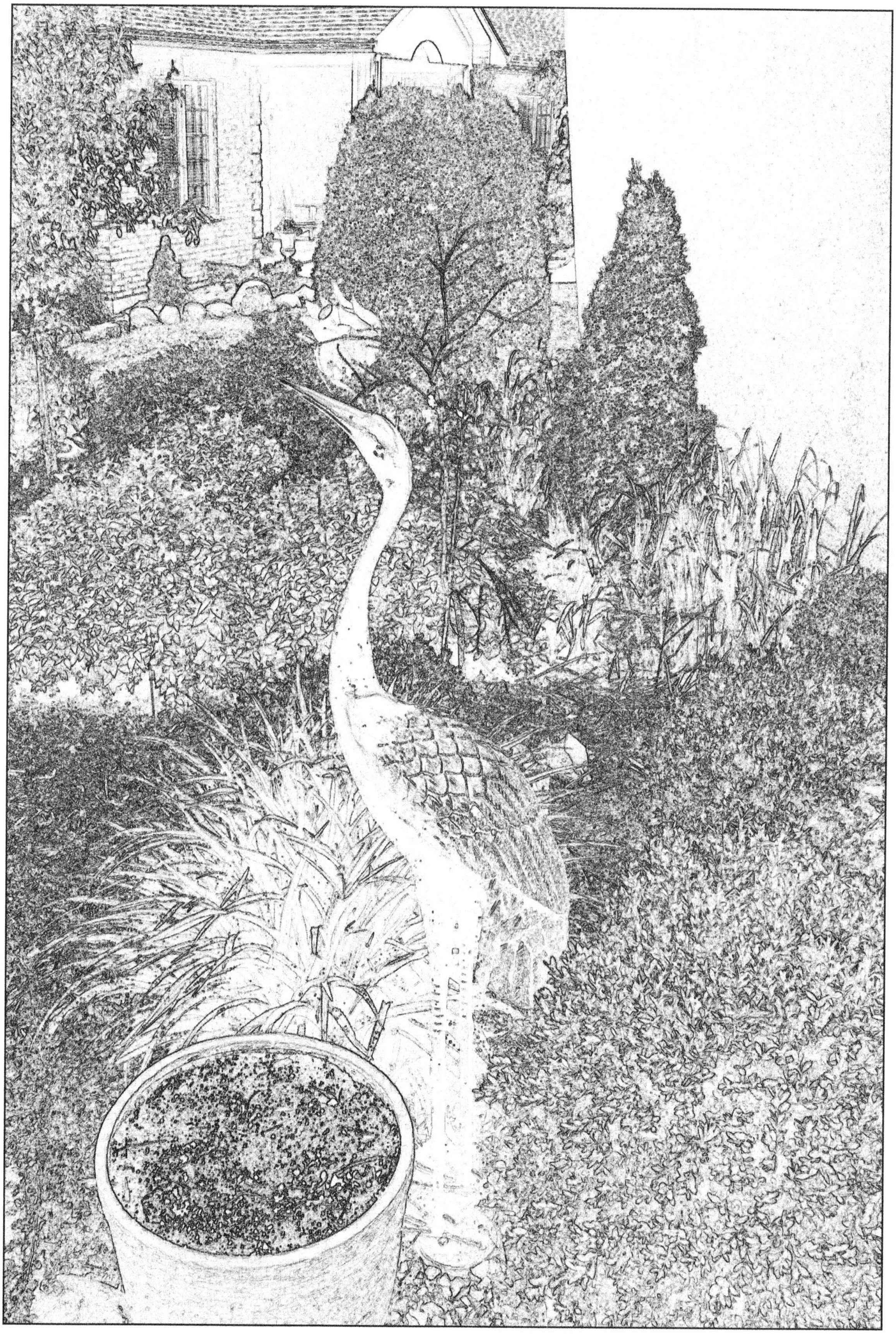

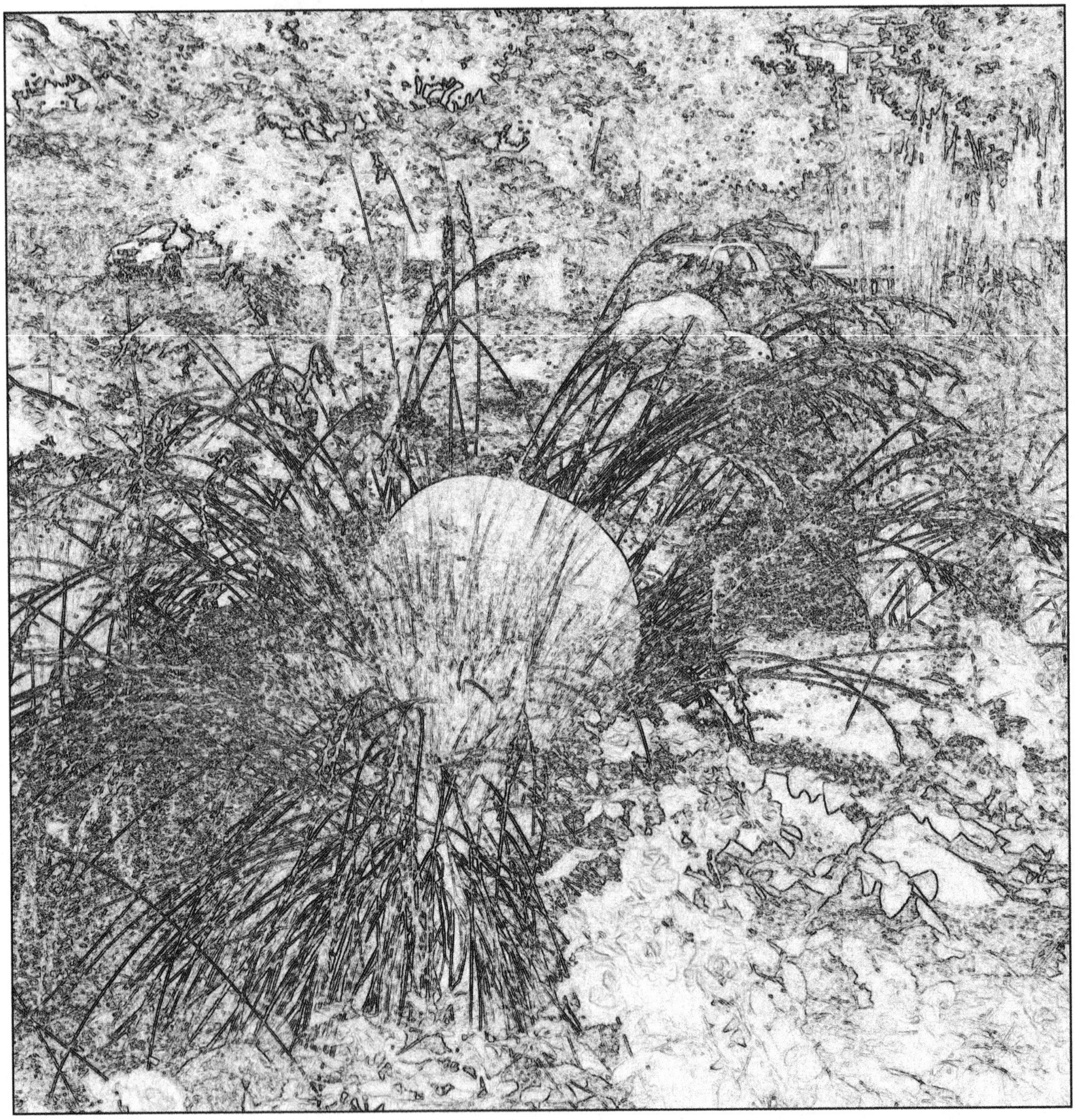

The Winter Garden

The winter garden is a bonus! If you have selected a variety of trees and shrubs, both deciduous and evergreen, and mixed them with various perennials and perennial grasses, you will be able to enjoy the beauty of your garden throughout the winter season as well as spring, summer, and fall.

Even topped with snow and lacking the color of flowers, the contours of each planting in your garden provide a display of beauty. The silhouette of bare branches of deciduous trees and shrubs juxtaposed against fully-formed evergreens are quite showy, and when branches are red, they add even more impact.

The dried stems of perennial flowers and grasses add even more dimension to your garden, and if you have included flowering specimen trees and left the fruit on, you will be able to enjoy the added beauty of their berries all winter long.

When designing your summer garden, keep these considerations in mind, and try to incorporate plantings that, although may be less colorful than your summer garden, pack a powerful punch in the winter garden.

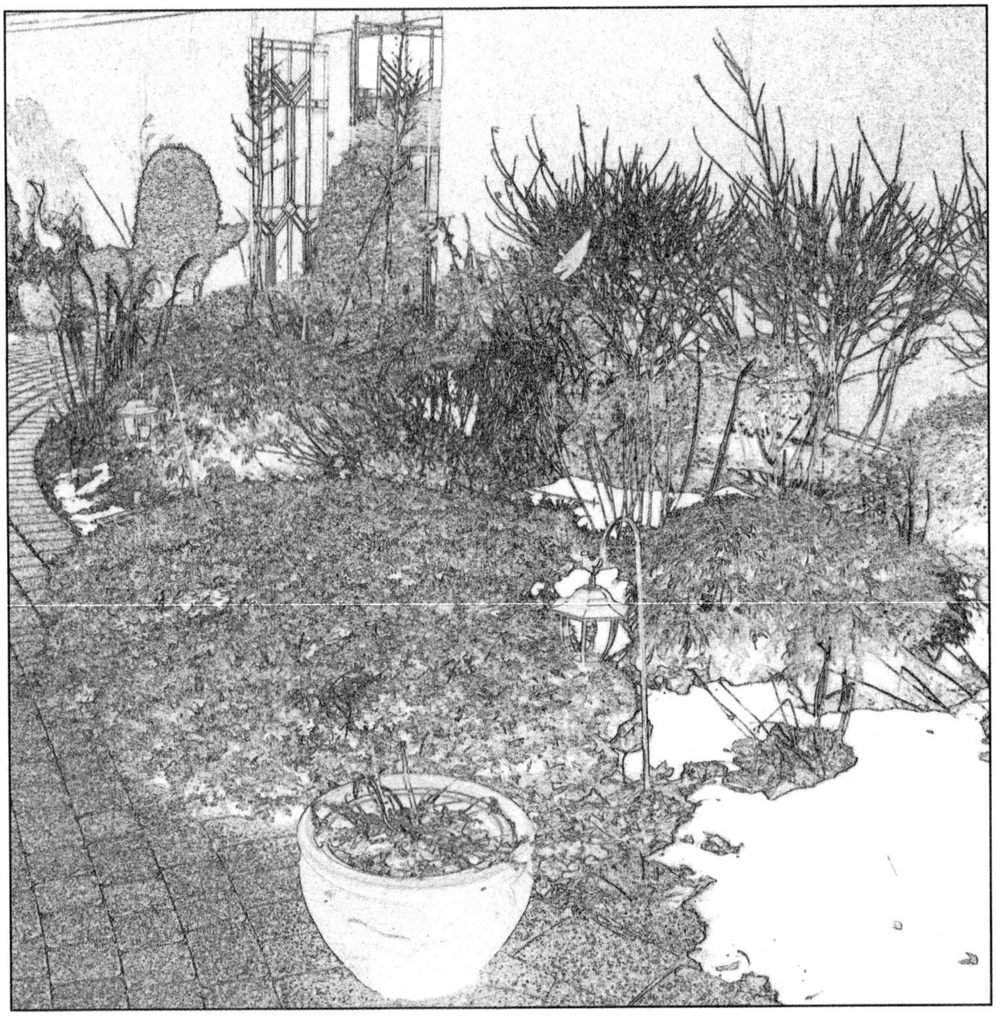

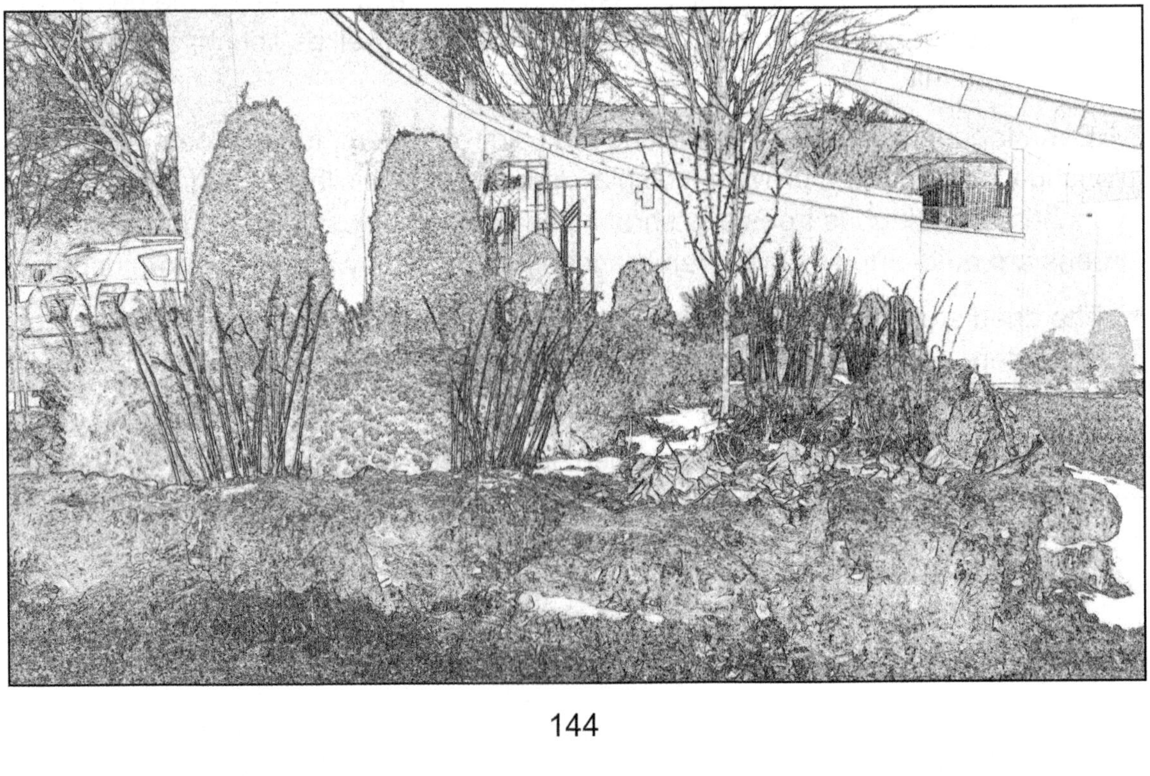

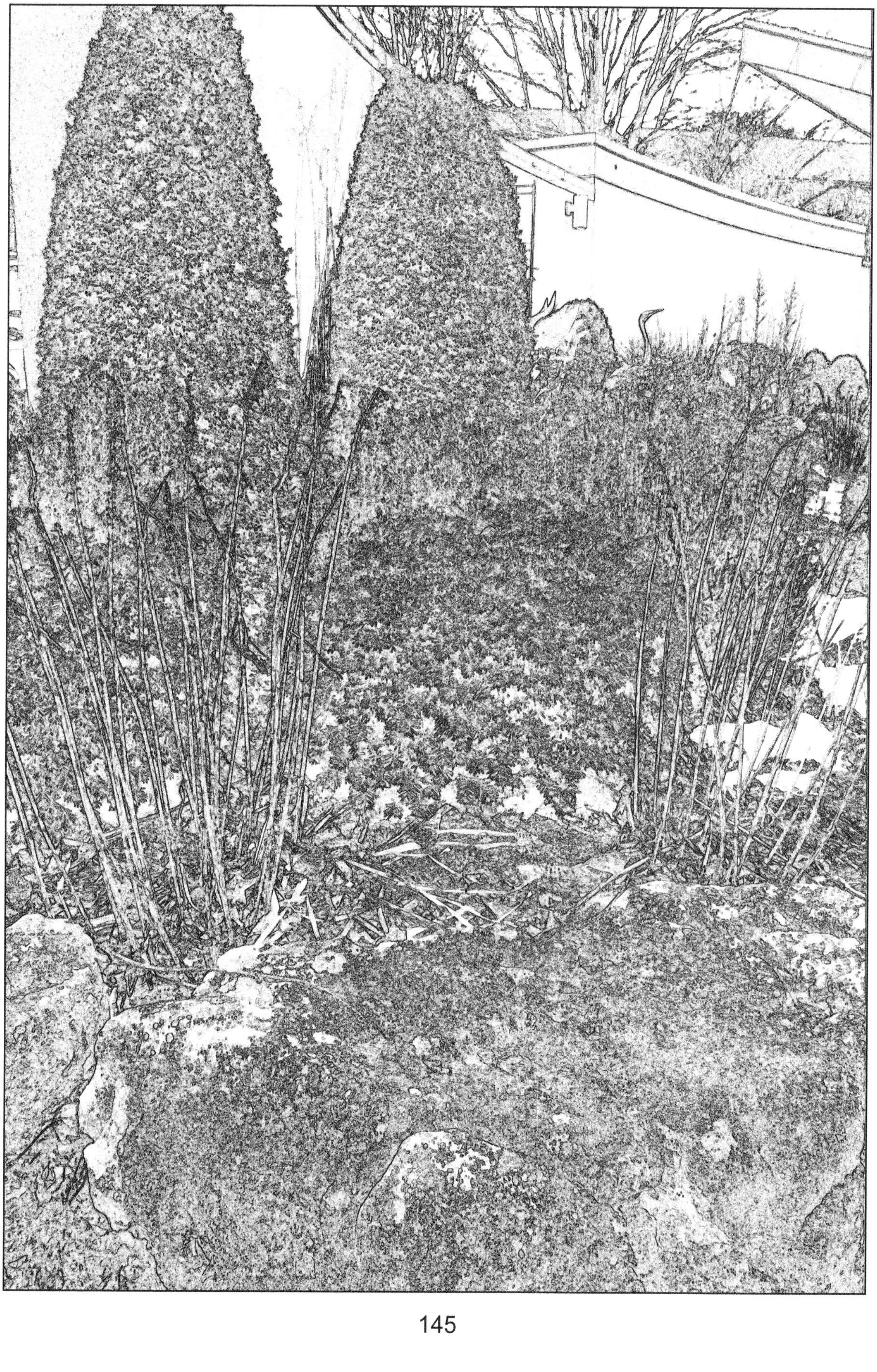

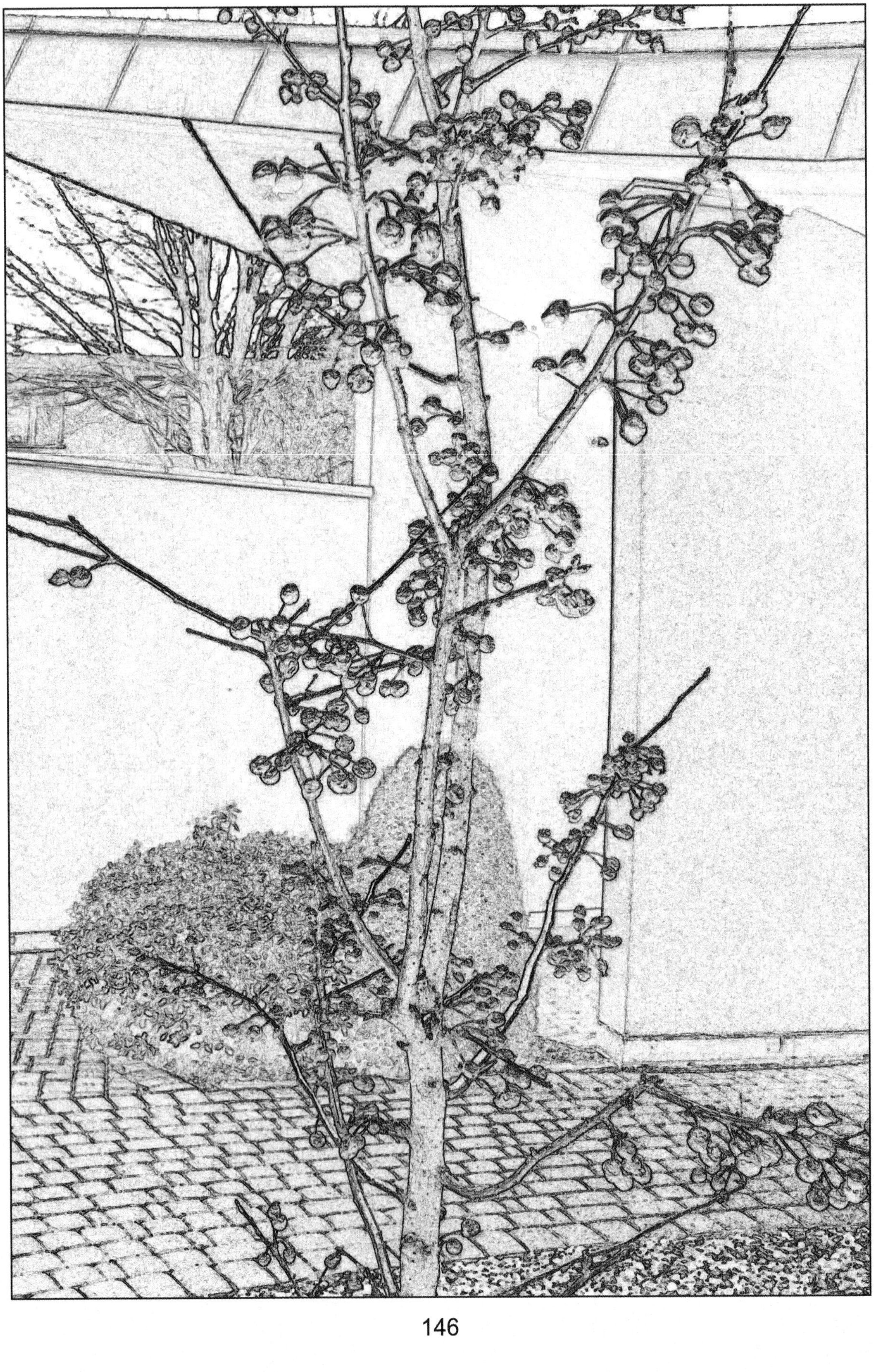

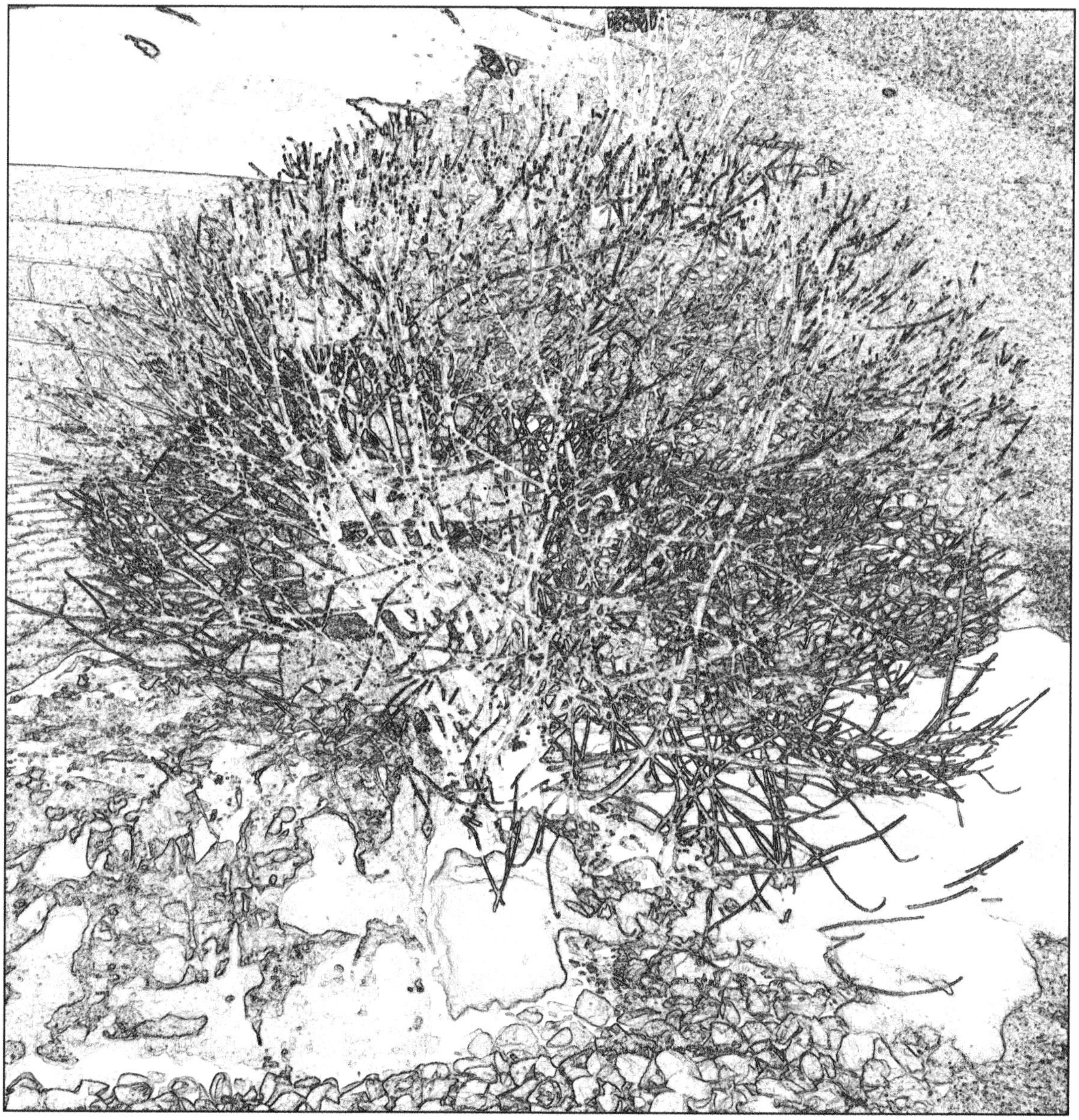

Developing A Landscape Plan

Now that you are familiar with the basics principles of landscape design, it is time to draw up a working plan. In order to do this, the property is measured as well as structures and existing hardscaping and a rough sketch from a bird's–eye-view of is drawn up. If your home sports a front porch, draw it in as well as an existing walkway and driveway as well as large trees and other elements you are planning to work around. Mark out dimensions of each element and draw a to-scale drawing. Use graph paper to draw to scale.

Before deciding on added hardscaping, consider sun and rain patterns. You will want to locate decks, patios, and the gazebo so that they are properly shaded and protected from the elements. Swimming pools are best located out in the open, away from deciduous trees and excessive plantings to keep leaves and debris out of them. The best location is in full sun to accommodate sunbathing and help keep water temperatures warm.

Once you have decided on the exact location of added hardscaping, map them out on your plan, drawing to scale.

Keeping in mind the basic elements of design already studied regarding plant choices, refer to your tree, shrub, and plant charts to make your selection. Once you have chosen your specimens, refer to the Plant Symbol chart for suggestions on how to illustrate each plant. Draw up your own version of symbols in the sizes you want to use within your design plan, move them around and experiment with them until you are satisfied with their positioning.

To help you get started with plotting out your plantings on a design plan, study the following series of garden design to give you a better understanding of concepts studied before choosing plantings that best suit your site.

Plant Symbols

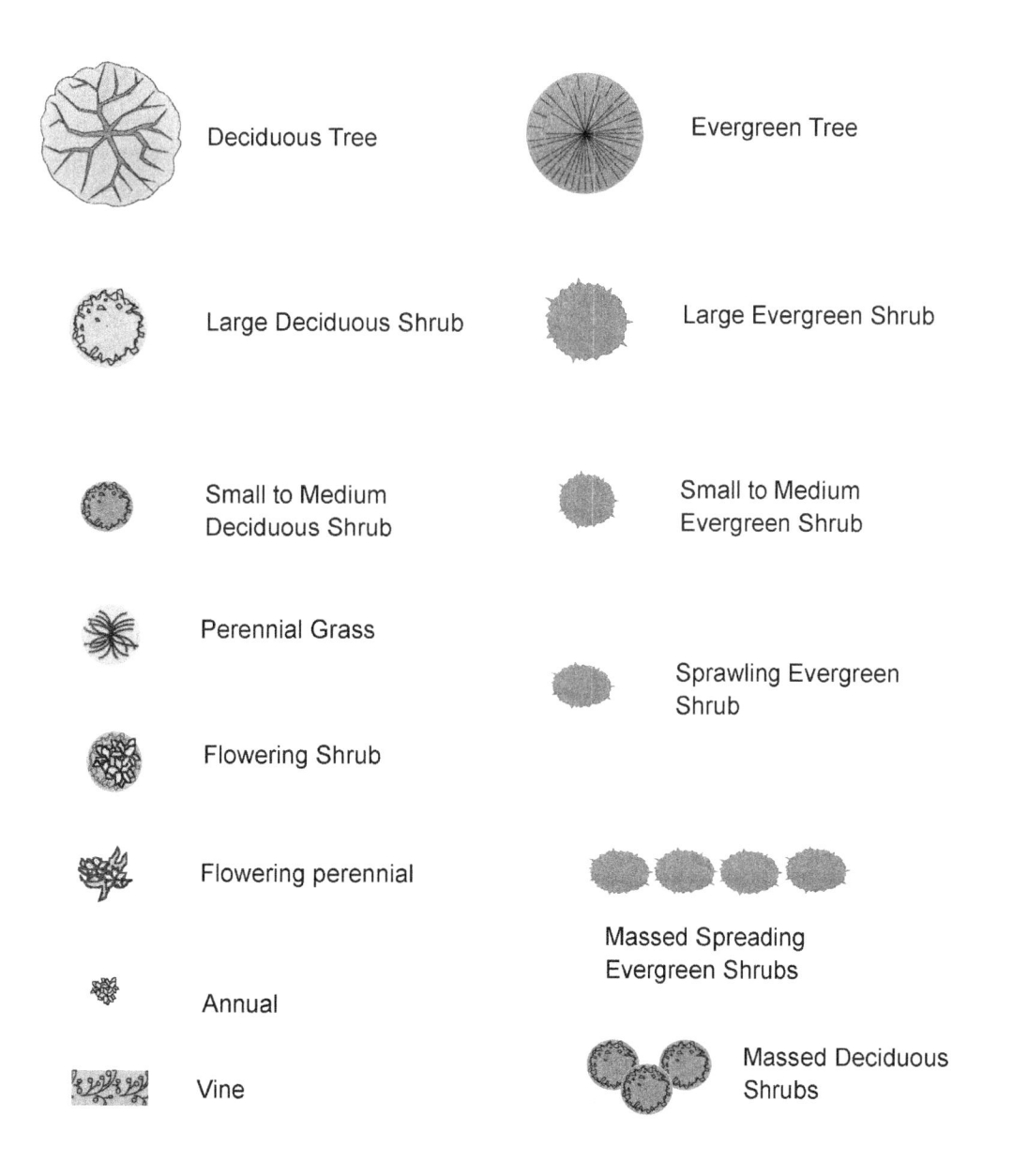

Deciduous Tree

Evergreen Tree

Large Deciduous Shrub

Large Evergreen Shrub

Small to Medium Deciduous Shrub

Small to Medium Evergreen Shrub

Perennial Grass

Sprawling Evergreen Shrub

Flowering Shrub

Flowering perennial

Massed Spreading Evergreen Shrubs

Annual

Vine

Massed Deciduous Shrubs

COTTAGE ADDITIONS

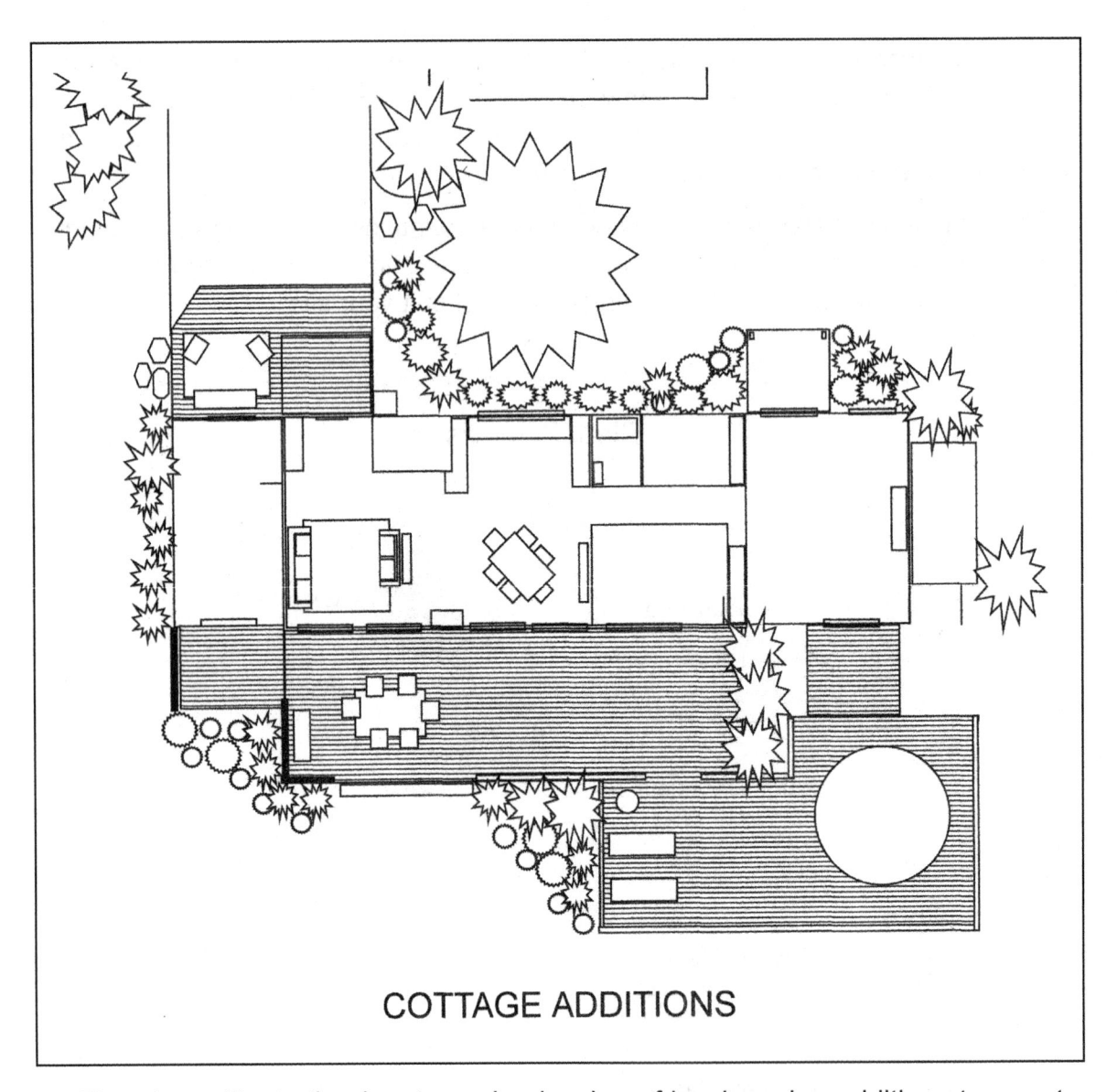

The above illustration is a to-scale–drawing of hardscaping additions to a cottage. An above-ground swimming pool was added to the lake-side as well as decking around it adjacent to an existing deck with access from the great room. This deck was raised up to accommodate the height of the pool. To completely enclose this area, a solid wood fence was added to an outside corner for a wind break and backdrop for lounge chairs, and open railing designed to code with locked entrance from a gate surrounds the rest of the deck.

A second deck was added from a walkout door off the master bedroom. A stretch of fencing acts as a wind break and to provide privacy. A large extension of decking was added to the front deck at the front entrance. This addition steps down from the original section and designates a comfortable seating area.

Trees, shrubs, and perennials were added to the plan to soften the edges of all hardscaping.

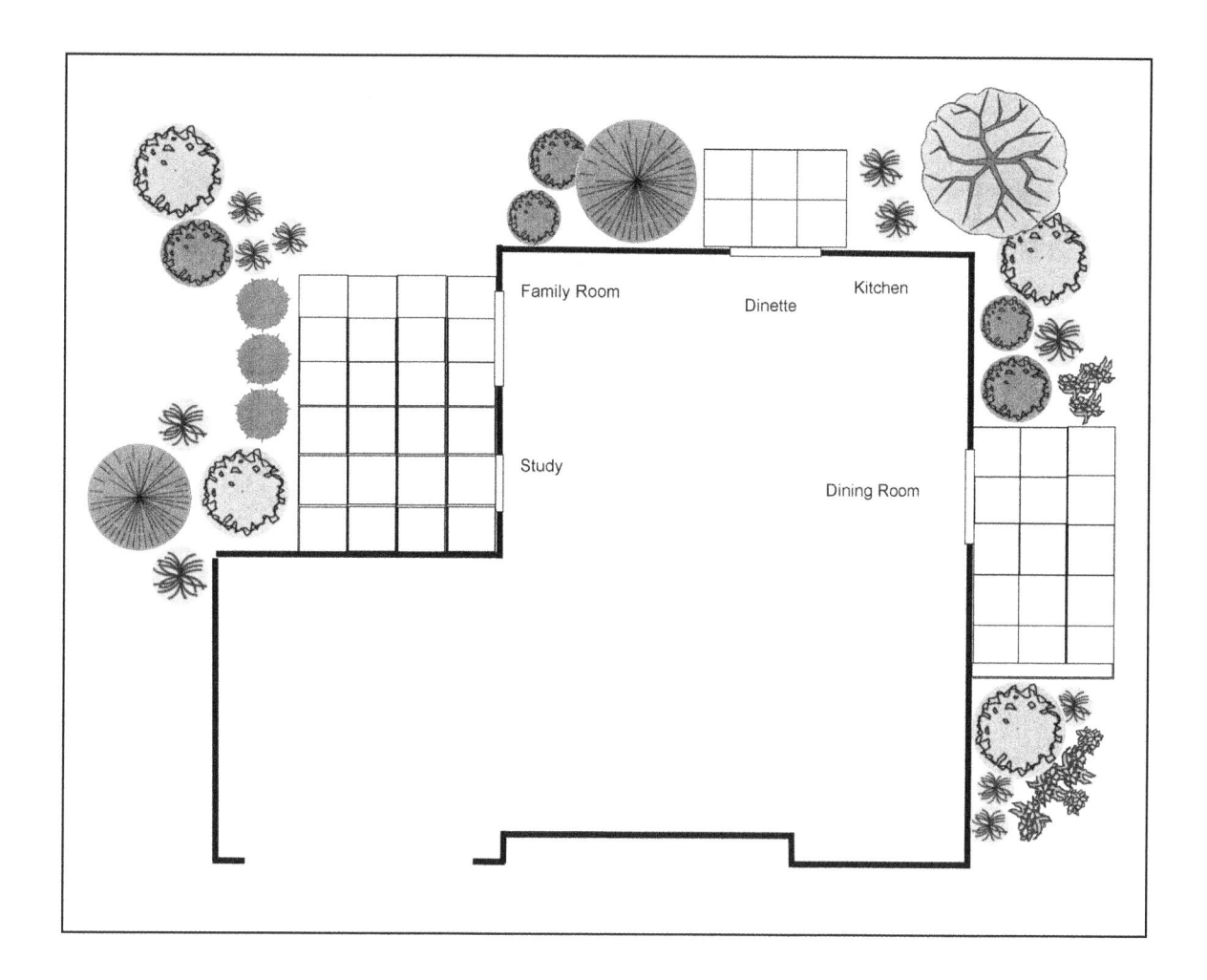

Hardscaping in this illustration includes the addition of patio extending from the dining room, dinette, and family room. To maintain privacy from the front view of the home, the dining room patio is partitioned off with a section of high fence. All patio areas are enclosed by the planting of garden beds to further distinguish each space.

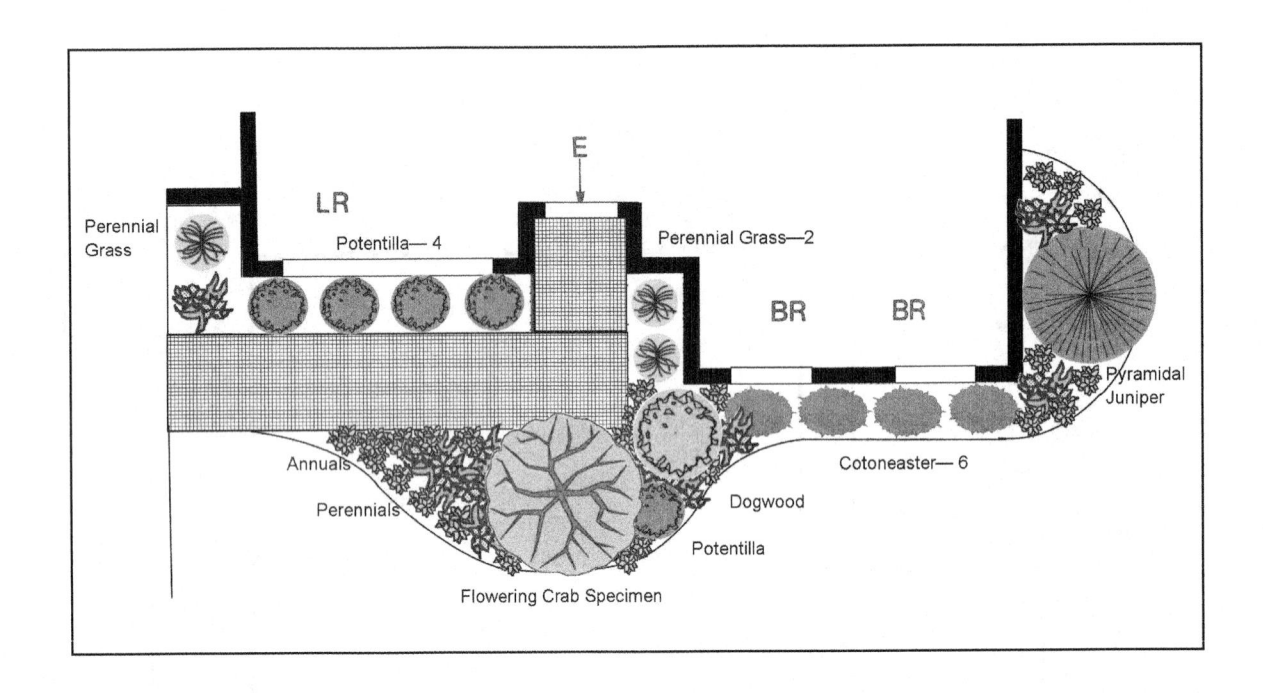

Hardscaping to this front entrance includes two sections of walkway, the first level with the driveway, and the second a step up higher to the front door. Planting beds flow along the walkway and continue across the front of the home and around the side to visually expand the width of the home and soften outside corners. Larger plantings are centered into the planting beds and lower plantings are stepped down and away from them causing the eye to be directed along the length of the beds. Note that low-spreading specimens are planted beneath windows so as not to block the view. Tall perennial grasses are planted against solid sections of wall to break the height.

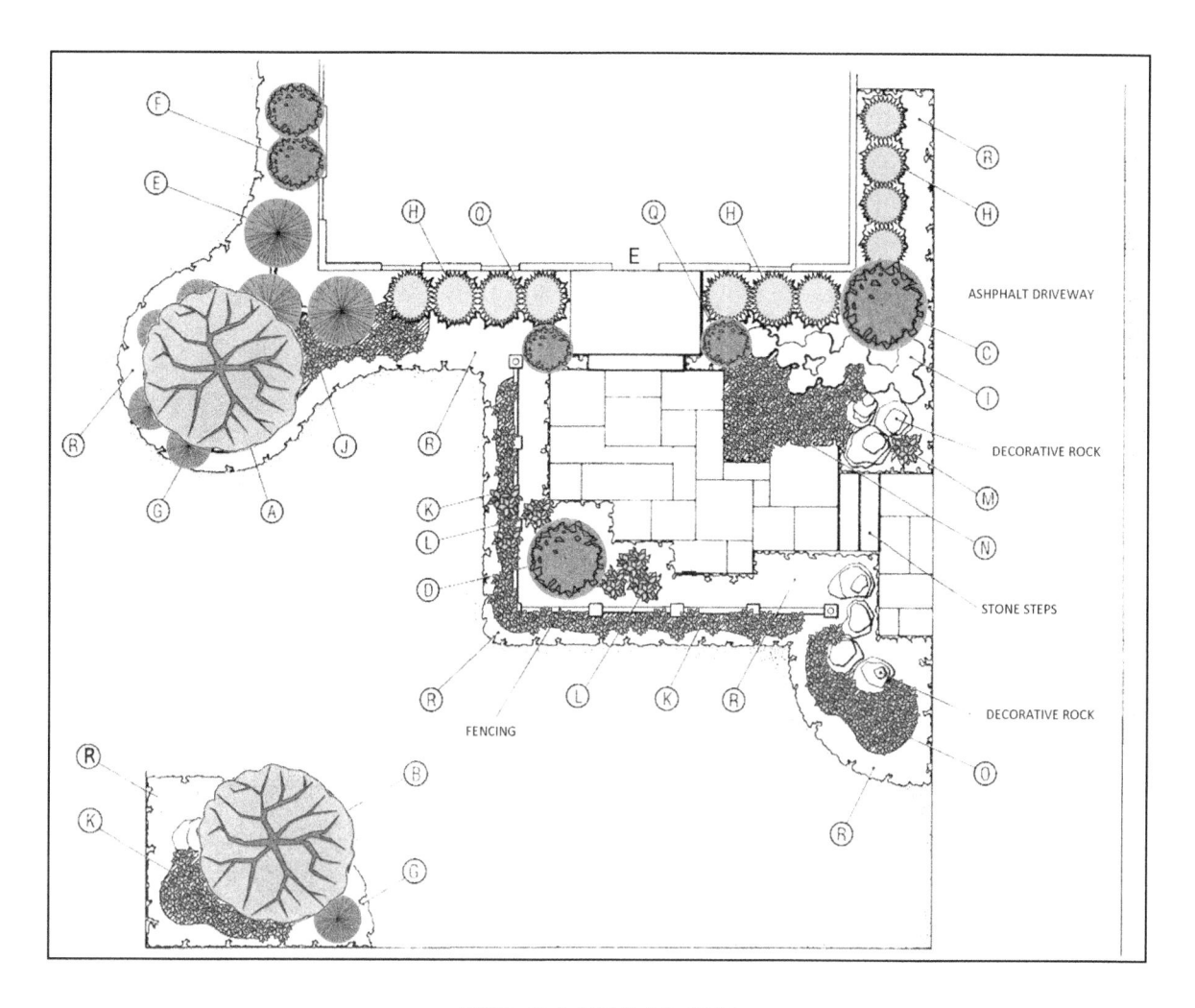

FRONT YARD

- A. Dwarf Crab-apple
- B. Decorative Pear Tree
- C. Purple-leaf Sand cherry
- D. Silver-leaf Dogwood
- E. Hydrangea
- F. Spirea
- G. Mugo Pine
- H. Boxwood
- I. Wintercreeper (Euonymus)
- J. – Q. Flowering Perennial
- R. Ground cover

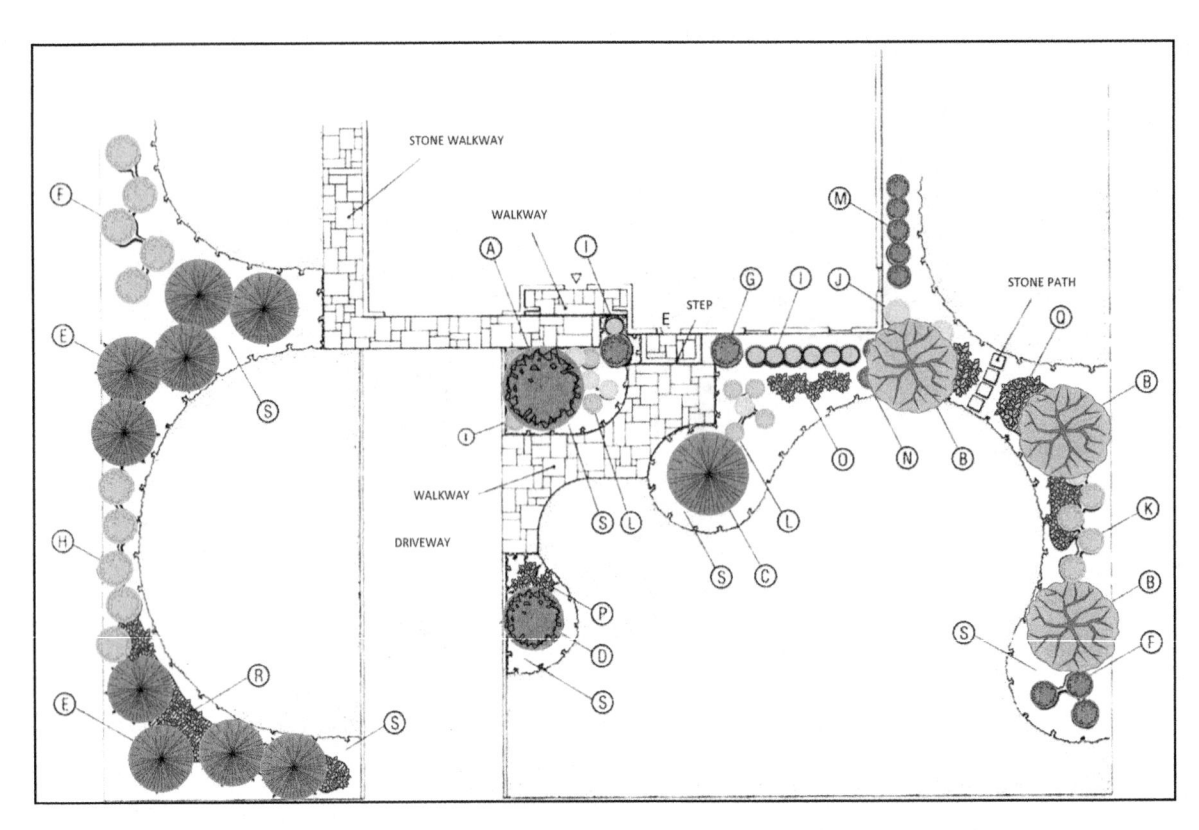

ADVANCED FRONT YARD

A.	Purple-leaf Sand Cherry
B.	Serviceberry
C.	Yew
D.	Lilac
E.	Juniper
F.	Spirea
G.	Japanese Pieris
H.	Spirea
I.	Mugo Pine
J.	Potentilla
K.	Potentilla
L.	Potentilla
M.	Cotoneaster
N.	Spirea
O.—R.	Perennial
S.	Ground Cover

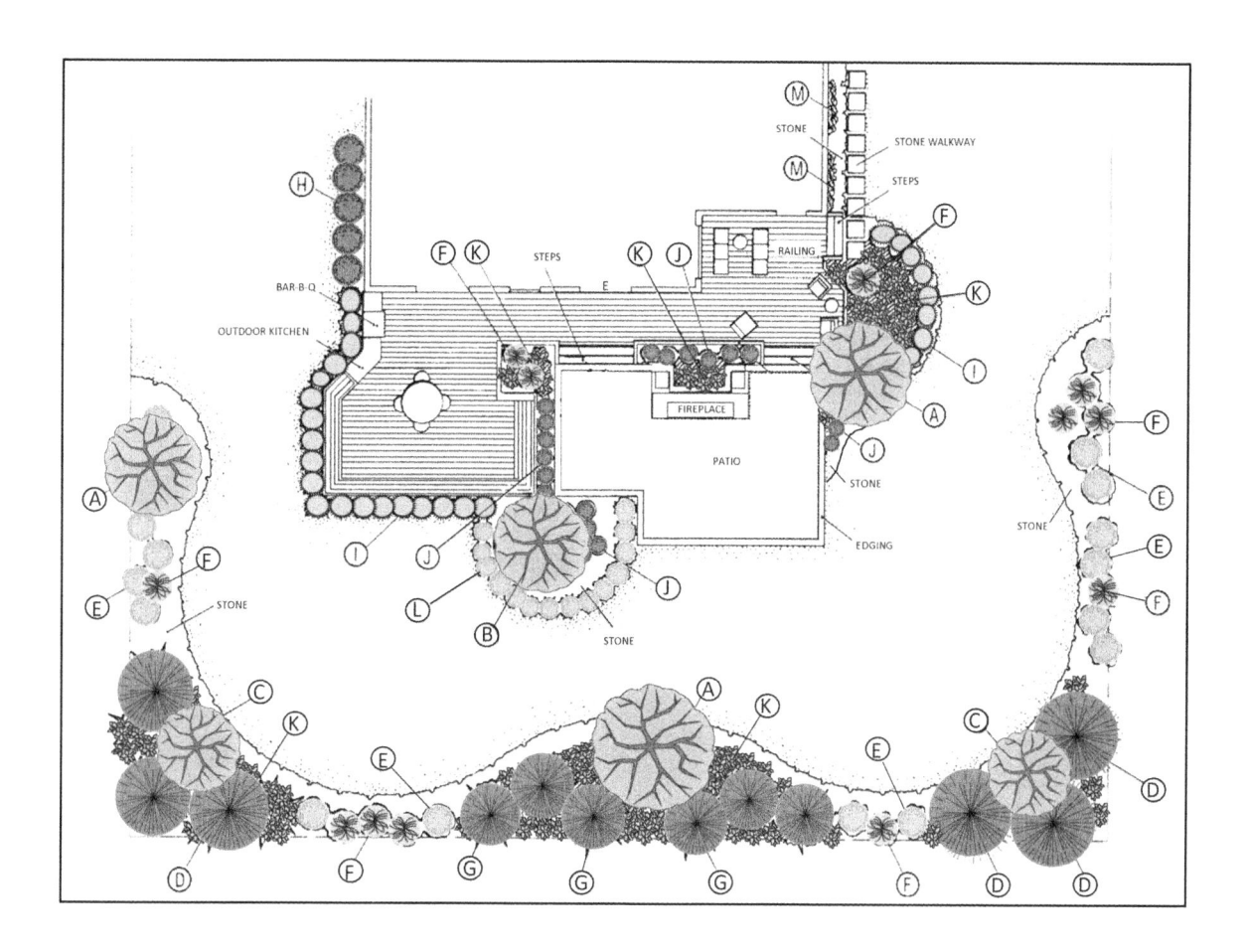

ADVANCED BACK YARD

- A. River Birch
- B. Flowering Crab Apple
- C. French Lilac Standard
- D. Upright Yew
- E. Spirea
- F. Ornamental Grass
- G. Globe Cedar
- H. Potentilla
- I. Mugo Pine
- J. Boxwood
- K. Perennials
- L. Bergenia
- M. Climbing Honeysuckle

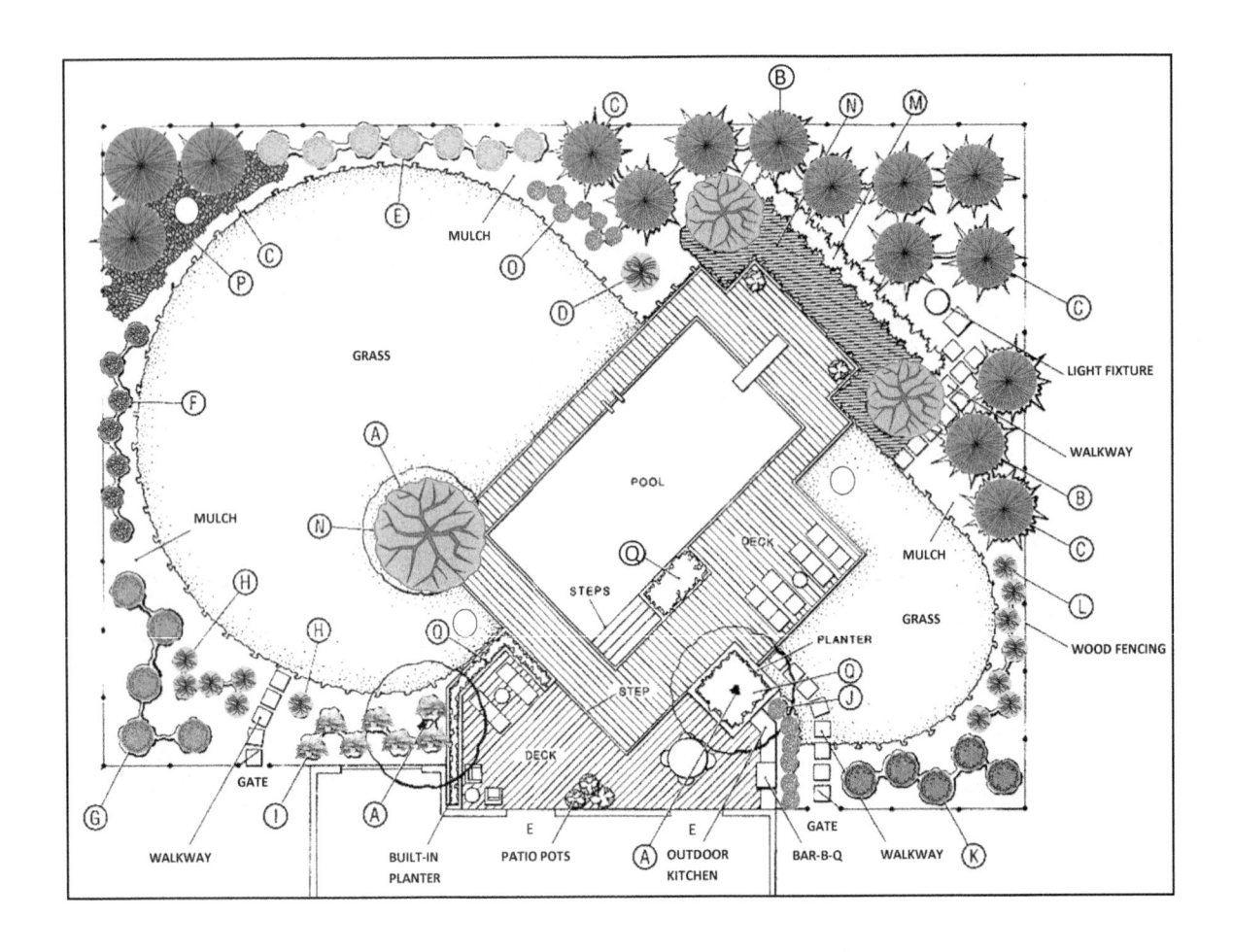

ADVANCED BACK YARD WITH POOL

A.	River Birch	K.	Potentilla
B.	Flowering Crab Apple	L.	Ornamental Grass
C.	Pyramidal Cedar	M.	Japanese Blood Grass
D.	Yucca	N.	Flowering Ground Cover
E.	Spirea	O.	Bergenia
F.	Rose of Sharon	P.	Flowering Perennials
G.	Japanese Barberry	Q.	Flowering Annuals
H.	Ornamental Grass		
I.	Hosta		
J.	Bergenia		

CPSIA information can be obtained
at www.ICGtesting.com
Printed in the USA
LVOW03s2035140316
479106LV00035B/578/P

9 781492 818113